Kathryn Kuhlman

The Radio Chapel Years

Shane Philpott

Tulsa, OK

18 17 16 15 10 9 8 7 6 5 4 3 2 1

Kathryn Kuhlman: The Radio Chapel Years
ISBN 13: 978-168031-045-0
Copyright © 2015 by Shane Philpott
Published by Harrison House Publishers

CONTENTS

ACKNOWLEDGEMENTS

First and foremost, I would like to thank God. In the process of putting this book together I came to realize just how amazing His providence has been in my life. God has given me the opportunity to pursue my passions and the power to believe in my dreams. I could never have done this without the faith I have in Him, the Almighty God.

I am forever thankful and indebted to Keith and Mary Williams for the selfless sharing of their experiences and resources with me, and the sincere and valuable encouragement that they extended to me during our times together. I look forward to fellowshipping with them again in Heaven. I am a better man for their friendship.

I want to recognize my wife, Lisa, for both her unwavering support and countless hours of editing and proofreading the numerous manuscripts necessary to bring this project to pass. Her continual encouragement kept me steady and focused throughout this journey.

I am extremely grateful to the congregation of Christian Fellowship Church for their strong support and encouragement as I pursued this labor of love. They alone know the story behind the story and the price that was paid to walk upon this path.

I place on record my deep sense of gratitude for Rev. Kenneth and Lynette Hagin, Rev. Mark Barclay, Rev. Dean Brown, Rev. Greg Squires and Rev. Bill Tvedt for their friendship and unceasing encouragement, support, wisdom, and guidance.

I wish to express my sincere thanks to Rev. Tony Cooke for thinking of me and introducing me to the great people at Harrison House Publishers.

I am very proud of my son, Josiah Philpott, for his editing and cover design contributions.

I am grateful to Terry Harrison, Historian Archivist with the Lee P. Loomis Archives and Mason City Public Library Genealogy Collection, for the many historical documents and photographs he provided for this venture.

I am appreciative of Wayne E. Warner, author of *Kathryn Kuhlman: The Woman Behind the Miracles*, for generously supplying many of the legal documents that were essential to the compilation of this book.

I would like to take this opportunity to express my gratitude to Gladys Schott, the administrator of Keith Williams Ministries, for her sacrificial help and support.

I also place on record my sense of gratitude to one and all, which directly or indirectly, have lent their hand to this venture.

Finally, I want recognize my incredible children, Josiah, Brianna, Johnny, Lily Anna, Roman, and London. You are remarkable, and I will always purpose to be a Dad you can be proud of, in this life and the life to come.

DEDICATION

For my wife, Lisa.

You believed in me.

And we know that God causes all things to work together for good to those who love God, to those who are called according to His purpose.

Romans 8:28 (NASB)

INTRODUCTION

And Jesus said to them, "Therefore every scribe who has become a disciple of the kingdom of heaven is like a head of a household, who brings out of his treasure things new and old."

Matthew 13:52 (NASB)

This is not a history book. It is a treasure chest. Like rare and valuable gems buried long ago, now unearthed, the early years of Kathryn Kuhlman's ministry prove as equally precious. From July 1937 through May 1939, Kathryn both ministered at and presided over Radio Chapel, a grand ministry of evangelism, revival, and salvation located in the Heartland of America.

Radio Chapel was a church unlike any other. It was pioneered in Mason City, Iowa, in 1937 by Burroughs Waltrip, the "Louisiana Pulpiteer," and Kathryn Kuhlman, the "Girl Evangelist," and quickly became a powerful ministry base of revival and one of the most spectacular non-denominational churches to grace the American landscape of that day.

Burroughs came to the Heartland with a dream of bringing salvation to thousands through his dynamic and unique end-time preaching. Kathryn, meanwhile, was making massive strides in the Pentecostal movement as the passionate, yet eloquent pastor of the famed Denver Revival Tabernacle. For a brief time, Burroughs and Kathryn, who would marry in 1938, took America's Heartland by

1

storm and shook its religious foundations. These were some of the earliest, most obscure and misunderstood years of Kathryn's ministry. These were known as her Radio Chapel years.

At the height of Radio Chapel's success, the church was conducting services six days a week, broadcasting daily over the radio, and hosting both national and international speakers. Attendance at these services could run upward of one thousand people per night with dozens of decisions for Christ following every meeting.

Kathryn was effectively pastoring and preaching at two churches: one in Mason City, Iowa, and the other in Denver, Colorado—frequently traveling the distance of almost 800 miles to serve both congregations. Radio Chapel published its own monthly magazine and routinely pursued evangelistic outreaches in the surrounding states and country. It truly lived up to its label, "The Most Unique Church in the World."

Radio Chapel's spectacular beginning was eclipsed only by its thunderous collapse. Saddled with immense debt, a lawsuit, governmental opposition, strife from surrounding churches and souring public opinion, it was over as quickly as it had begun. All of this transpired in a short span of just twenty-three months. It is well known that the marriage between Burroughs and Kathryn later ended in divorce in April 1947. After their divorce, Burroughs quickly faded into obscurity, eventually disappearing and never to be heard from again by either family or friends. As for Kathryn, she went on to achieve international honor and recognition as one of the most influential faith preachers of the Twentieth Century.

To dismiss Kathryn's life and ministry before or during her marriage and divorce would be unwise. We would not so easily dismiss the life of Moses before he slew the Egyptian, the life of David before he committed adultery with Bathsheba, or the life of Peter before he denied the Lord Jesus Christ. The greatest lessons to be learned are the ones gleaned from the lives of those who fought the ever-present fight between good and evil, light and darkness, right and wrong. Life can become dark at times, yet great and mighty things can come out of those darkest seasons.

This book is the untold redemptive story of those great and mighty things. Within these covers have been assembled a wonderful compilation of letters, articles, messages, and sermon notes from Kathryn Kuhlman's earliest days while at Radio Chapel. Were it not for God's amazing providence and divine appointments, this body of work would have been lost to history, quite possibly forever.

Kathryn emerged from the darkest season of her life to become one of the brightest lights the American church has witnessed in modern ministry times. She was a faith pioneer, and the secrets to her victorious life and overcoming faith are seen in these beloved documents that she had the pleasure of authoring, co-authoring, influencing, teaching, and preaching.

As your heart explores and discovers the enduring truths of these intimate writings, it is my prayer that you will experience the true heartbeat and passion of Kathryn Kuhlman, and that her life and ministry might be an even greater inspiration to you in the years to come.

Chapter One

HIDDEN TREASURES

It is the glory of God to conceal things, but the glory of kings is to search things out.

Proverbs 25:2 (ESV)

In the fall of 2005, a burden for my city was heavy upon my heart. As the pastor of Christian Fellowship Church in Mason City, Iowa, my congregation and I had been experiencing very different and unusually intense times of prayer in our services during the months of October and November. God was speaking. He had our attention and we were listening. Every church service brought with it an ever-increasing expectation and anticipation in the hearts of our members. It was tangible. It was real. It could be felt. Like a spiritual crescendo, there was a sense that something was building and was about to crest. Then it happened. At the close of our midweek service on Wednesday, November 30, while the congregation was deep in worship and prayer, I felt an urge in my spirit, a burden to speak and release prophetic words from God. It was strong. It was powerfully strong! And it could not be stopped. Almost immediately, prophetic revelation broke forth from the inside of me, setting the stage for the remarkable journey upon which I would soon embark.

"I will set right that which is wrong," spoke the Spirit of God, "and I will do that which has not been done, and together we will finish that which was begun. That which was begun years ago shall see its day and shall see its hour. It shall spring forth." The words poured out like water now. Heaven was open above me and hearts were open all around me. Men and women stood listening intently throughout the sanctuary, almost frozen at attention, as the Lord exhorted us. "Justice is Mine, and I will redeem from the hands of the enemy that which has been lost for decades, and I will bring it back in the seventieth year. As it was in the days of Daniel, so shall it be in your day." Hands began to lift in the sanctuary as people responded in worship to the holiness of the moment. There was such a ring to the words as they pierced the atmosphere with both clarity and authority. Then came these additional words through the Holy Spirit, "I will resurrect that which has been trodden in the mud. No man shall withstand it. No one shall hold it back. For this is My time, and this is My church, and this is My way. It shall happen on My appointed season. It shall spring forth. It shall spring from Heaven, and it shall do what I have called it to do."

THE SEARCH BEGINS

The congregation rejoiced together with me that evening with full knowledge that the Lord had deposited something precious and rare into our hearts. However, I privately admitted to myself that I had absolutely no idea what God was referring to with His prophetic words to our church. Stepping off of the stage and exiting the sanctuary, I found myself engrossed in prayer. It was almost like everything was suddenly now in slow motion all around me. I was mentally replaying the words that I had spoken just minutes earlier, and although the entire prophecy was amazing, it was the reference to the seventy years that stuck in my mind like a splinter. "I will redeem from the hands of the enemy that which has been lost for decades, and I will bring it back in the seventieth year." What did that mean? Was this promise personally directed to me? Our church? The nation? There was no way I could be satisfied with not knowing.

I arrived in my study only to find myself staring out the window into the November night. It was quiet now, which allowed me the time and space needed to reflect and listen to God. I was not able to put into words why my heart was so stirred over the past few weeks, nor could I yet explain that evening's prophetic utterance. Still, I knew there was a divine plan and purpose to what had just taken place. "I will bring it back in the seventieth year," was what the Lord had said to me. Meditating on that particular phrase, the mathematics of the years began to take shape in my mind: 2005 minus 70 years was 1935. Was there some type of significant event which had taken place in Mason City during the 1930's?

Just then, I felt my attention being pulled to a bookcase directly to the right of where I was standing. At that very instant, the title of a book that had been given to me years ago seemed to light up and literally jump out from among the others. The providence of

God began to manifest as the pieces of the puzzle started to fall into place. The book was *Daughter of Destiny: Kathryn Kuhlman ... Her Story*, by Jamie Buckingham, which was published in 1976. A fellow minister had given the book to me shortly after my wife and I pioneered Christian Fellowship Church in September 1993. The very moment my fingertips touched the cover, I straightaway recalled the chapters within which briefly described Kathryn's season of ministry in Mason City, Iowa. That was it! I immediately connected with the mind of God and my heart leaped inside my chest as I anxiously removed the book from the shelf. I now knew what this burden on my heart was, and I knew that it had to do with Kathryn's ministry while she was in my city in the 1930's. As a result of the specifics of the prophecy, I promptly realized there must be so much more to the story that had previously been told, and I also knew by the Spirit of God that the time had finally arrived to reveal what was unknown. It was time to set the story straight and make things right.

Kathryn Kuhlman was a faith pioneer. She was a woman, whom to this day, continues to be one of the most loved, appreciated, and respected preachers of the Twentieth Century. Even after her death in Tulsa, Oklahoma, on February 20, 1976, her life and ministry evoke feelings of deep admiration from those who cherish her memory. Like many others before me, I had read about Kathryn's time in Mason City with great fascination. Whether it was her marriage to and subsequent divorce from Burroughs Waltrip, the pioneering and collapse of Radio Chapel, or her personal struggles throughout those trying times, there seemed to be no shortage of tribulation for Kathryn to overcome in her ministry's earliest years. As a result, there seemed to be an unspoken reluctance to discuss that part of her life and an almost disdain for that season of time, a season which I believed undoubtedly contained valuable life lessons to be gleaned. Now, as a result of our church service, I knew the time had come.

Reflecting further on the words of the prophecy from our service, I contemplated the references made to Daniel and the seventy years. Daniel was a chosen man, a prophet of God who was taken into captivity by the Babylonians. It was following a time of intense prayer that Daniel turned his attention to the writings of the prophet Jeremiah. The Book of Jeremiah records that he foresaw the day when, after seventy years, the children of Israel would experience deliverance from their captors. Consequently, it became clear to Daniel that the seventy-year time period was about to end, signaling God was about to move on His peoples' behalf. Likewise, I myself could now see the parallel that God was about to do something great as I began to realize the spiritual correlation.

I was fully aware of how important it would be to follow my heart regarding everything that was unfolding before my very eyes. I definitely felt the Lord had opened a door, even a divine opportunity, and one that could only be understood through faith and obedience. But the question remained, where do I begin? I took Jamie Buckingham's book home with me that night and reread the two chapters titled, "The Slaying of the Egyptian" and "The Bush Burns," which were dedicated to Kathryn's short time of ministry while in Mason City.

There were so many unanswered questions. So many loose ends. So much uncertainty connected to this pivotal and difficult time in Kathryn's life. What brought her to Mason City? What part did she play in the pioneering of Radio Chapel? What was her style of ministry during those years? What brought her through the valley's depths? What about her mountaintops and victories? And being that this season of her life was so immensely crucial to the development of her ministry, what lessons could be learned from her experiences? My mind was overrun with these types of questions.

Early the next morning I told my wife I was going to begin at the public library. I did not know where else to start this journey. I wasn't exactly sure the extent of history the library would have on hand concerning Mason City, but I felt it was at least worth the effort. Prayerfully searching through history had worked for Daniel, and I had faith it would work for me as well. At a minimum, perhaps someone there could point me in the right direction. Little did I know the vast wealth of information and history that God was preparing to place in my hands. Needless to say, I began this venture with no small amount of excitement coupled with a heartfelt respect for this charge that God had laid so strongly upon my heart.

The Mason City Public Library is a place that transports you back in time. The facility itself is reminiscent of those old historical buildings that you might see in the curled and yellowed photographs of days gone by. I believed I was in the right place and I felt strongly that Kathryn's season at Radio Chapel would be the place to start. Stopping at the front desk, I enquired of the staff as to what type of historical archives might be available for study. The lady kindly referred me to the historical room, informing me that daily editions of the local newspapers from the 1930's were accessible on microfiche. With notebook and pen in hand, I pulled a rickety chair up to the old microfiche machine and went to work. The dozens of metal drawers in the microfiche station contained hundreds of boxed reels of film labeled with the dates of days long gone. It wasn't long before I uncovered a multitude of articles with such titles as "Young Blond Evangelist Arrives at Radio Chapel" and "America's Outstanding Young Woman Evangelist." I spent the better part of the next two months in that historical room, slowly unearthing the timeline and history of Radio Chapel and striking gold by eventually compiling over one hundred articles related to Kathryn Kuhlman and Radio Chapel. Over the course of time, my research yielded another fifty articles from a dozen additional regional and national newspaper publishers from as far away as Texas, Ohio, and Alabama. Throughout this entire process, the Lord kept bringing to remembrance the words of Proverbs 25:2, *"The glory of kings is to search out a matter." (NASB)*

It was during this amazing time of exploration that I had the opportunity to get to know and work with the city historian employed by the library. It was clear that he both loved and breathed the rich history of our city, and was well versed in the facts and timeline of Radio Chapel as well. Radio Chapel, it seemed, was quite the legend in Mason City. Over the next few weeks, my research continued to grow as a number of photographs from Kathryn's Radio Chapel days were added to my materials. These images opened a window into the past and painted a canvas with an incredible picture that was beginning to form.

A DIVINE APPOINTMENT

One day while meeting with the historian, he asked me if I had ever attempted to locate or speak with Keith and Mary Williams, the former assistant pastors at Radio Chapel. Having previously seen photographs of Keith and Mary, which were taken at the time of their ordination service conducted by Burroughs and Kathryn in February, 1938, I was familiar with the young faces of whom he was referring. He then walked over to one of his cabinets and began to shuffle through the papers. Turning around, he handed me a note he had written from the early 1990's that contained the Williams' contact information for their ministry that was located in Watertown, South Dakota. He said that he had always intended to make contact with Keith and Mary to get more of the story behind Radio Chapel, yet never got around to it. He then offered me the chance to try it for myself. But it was now 2006. Almost seventy years had passed since the events surrounding Radio Chapel and Kathryn's ministry alongside Keith and Mary Williams. I had never considered that Keith and Mary might still be alive, let alone be able to be located. I was about to be pleasantly surprised.

After returning to my office at the church later that day and with telephone in hand, I took a deep breath and prayed. "Lord, let this be a divine appointment. Let me make contact with this precious couple. Grant me this opportunity to spend time with living history. Let it be Your will for a great window to open into the past and let me discover that which has for so long been hidden and forgotten." I dialed the number. After what seemed like an eternity, a wonderful lady by the name of Gladys answered the phone with the words, "Keith Williams Ministries." My heart stopped. I was literally sitting on the edge of my chair. There are times in life when you know everything is coming together and the pieces are falling into place. This was such a time! There is nothing sweeter than being in the center of God's plan.

I explained to Gladys to the best of my ability who I was and what I was searching for. There was really no other way to say it: I was looking for Keith and Mary Williams and quite honestly, I was hoping they were still alive. Keith was the man whom Kathryn laid her ordaining hands upon while at Radio Chapel. He was the man who knelt at the altar before her so very long ago and received the charge from her for the ministry which would become the center of his life. Many times I had read the weathered *Globe Gazette* article dated February 26, 1938, where it was reported "Miss Kathryn Kuhlman took charge of the service and preached the sermon" the evening he was ordained. This man lived it. He carried the story within his heart. He shared in her anointing. Keith was there for it all.

Gladys came alive on the telephone. She shared about the Williams' ministry and their lifelong service to God. She spoke of Keith and Mary's fondness for their Radio Chapel days, their service alongside Burroughs and Kathryn, and the tenderness in their voices when recalling those events from so long ago. She told me of Keith's tour in the Korean War as a chaplain and of his subsequent lifelong ministry to the nation of the Philippines. She related to me the ministerial travels of his life that included the founding of two Bible colleges in the Philippines. She expounded on his great love for Radio Chapel and admiration for Burroughs and Kathryn, and how he owed his ministerial life to his service with them. Then she told me she was sitting at the table with both Keith and Mary as we spoke. I could hardly believe what I was hearing. We spoke for almost an hour that day, Gladys, Keith, and I. Keith was in his early 90's at the time of our first conversation, but he was sharp as a tack when he recalled the history of his life and ministry. It was almost like he was 22 years old once again and Kathryn had just placed her hands upon him. His passion and love for Radio Chapel overwhelmed me as he invited me again and again to come visit with them. How could I do anything else but accept? This is where the word of the Lord was leading me. I could not get to Watertown, South Dakota, fast enough.

PROVIDENCE

To walk out the plan of God is to be a part of something exceedingly special. When God puts a plan in motion, there are really only two options: Go with it or resist it. I was going to go with it. It truly felt like a river—a river of providence—was carrying me along as I made plans to travel to Watertown. My destination was set and I loaded up my vehicle for the long drive, assured in my heart that something great was about to happen. So it is with all the things of God.

On February 9, 2006, I pulled into the driveway of the Williams' residence in Watertown, South Dakota, on a bitterly cold and snowy morning. I found myself praising God openly as I contemplated the day that awaited me. The chain of events leading up to meeting with Keith and Mary was undoubtedly orchestrated by the One who overwhelmed our church service with His presence and prophetic direction just two months earlier. Gathering together my research from the past eight weeks, along with pictures of Radio Chapel and copies of newspaper articles about Kathryn Kuhlman, I made my way to the front door. I didn't even have the opportunity to knock. Standing at the window, peering out at me with a huge smile on his face, was a slim and elderly man. He whisked the door open, almost pulling me inside as he did, and he wrapped his arms around me as he began to weep. "Oh, Pastor Shane," he said, "I'm so glad you came to see me today. I have so much to tell you." This precious man was about to become a part of the great Radio Chapel story once again—and there was no question in my mind he had an incredible story to tell!

We fellowshipped and laughed and reminisced together for many hours on that cold Thursday in Watertown. Keith and Mary cried as they shared about Burroughs and Kathryn's departure from Mason City. Keith recounted how he received a call for him and Mary to come to Burroughs and Kathryn's room where they lived at the Hotel Hanford the evening before they were to leave Mason City for good. He shared how they hugged and cried with them as they said their goodbyes to one another and forgave one another for any transgressions, known or unknown. They were not only ministry companions, they were best friends, and that final goodbye was so heart wrenching.

The four of them knelt together on the floor of that room at the Mason City Hotel Hanford, and they took turns praying for one another. They prayed for one another's futures and one another's ministries and they gave God thanks for their friendship and the rich times of fellowship they enjoyed. As they stood to their feet, Burroughs told Keith that he and Kathryn had a parting gift for their young son in the faith. Kathryn retrieved from the credenza her worn, black leather Bible cover she brought from Denver, Colorado, and handed it to Keith. As Keith unzipped it, he quickly recognized many of the sermons that Burroughs and Kathryn had preached at Radio Chapel and during their many crusades, going back even to Kathryn's years at Denver Revival Tabernacle. Pressed between the sermon notes was the white feather Kathryn wore while she preached and the Radio Chapel bookmark she used in her Bible. Keith said he wept as he tried to refuse their gift, strongly feeling the sermon outlines should stay with Burroughs and Kathryn. But of course, they insisted that their gift stay in the hands of Keith and Mary. Kathryn said it was the very best gift they could give—these messages of faith—to the young preacher. The holiness and power of that moment must have been overwhelming!

Digging for Treasure

Now almost seventy years later, as I shared in the precious memories of that evening, Keith suddenly stood to his feet. Abruptly turning around, he made his way to an old file cabinet in the corner of his office. There was purpose in his walk. As Mary continued sharing about that evening from so long ago, I couldn't take my eyes off of Keith in the corner of the room, hectically shuffling through papers and files in one of the drawers. Gladys made her way to Keith's side, asking him what it was he was looking for. He was a man on a mission now. He kept digging deeper and deeper into the various drawers and boxes, searching for something. Gladys returned to the table, not knowing what it was Keith might be searching for. A few more minutes passed before Keith came back to the table and handed me an old and worn Bible cover. With tears in his eyes, he asked me to open it. Slowly unzipping the leather cover, the treasure within was revealed. After all those years, almost seventy years since they were gifted, Burroughs Waltrip and Kathryn Kuhlman's sermon outlines saw the light of day once again. "I want you to have them," Keith said. I was at a loss for words as I simply stared at the sermon notes which I now held in my hands.

In her forty years of serving the Williams', Gladys had never seen those sermon outlines. Mary did not know Keith even still possessed them. There is really no way to appropriately describe an experience like that. In Matthew 13:52, Jesus said, "*Therefore every scribe who has become a disciple of the kingdom of heaven is like a head of a household, who brings out of his treasure things new and old."* (NASB). Keith had just brought out his old treasure.

Chapter Two

PIONEERING A DREAM CHURCH

I told them how the hand of my God had been favorable to me and also about the king's words which he had spoken to me. Then they said, "Let us arise and build." So they put their hands to the good work.

Nehemiah 2:18 (NASB)

It was clear from the onset that Burroughs Waltrip and Kathryn Kuhlman set out to create a dream ministry, the likes of which had never been seen. Together they launched a grand vision for evangelism, revival, and outreach to be directed from America's Heartland. On Sunday, July 18, 1937, Burroughs began a series of revival meetings that were held in the Mason City Armory. Kathryn, who was conducting multiple crusades in the Midwest at the time, made herself available for the commencement of the Mason City meetings. The Mason City *Globe Gazette* newspaper, which was reporting on the meetings, referred to Burroughs as a youthful southern evangelist known as the "Louisiana Pulpiteer" because of his dynamic evangelistic ministry in his home state. Herbert John, a prominent Minneapolis pianist and organist who also worked with Kathryn at various meetings, provided the music for the services. The newspaper referred to the meetings as a "citywide revival campaign." Burroughs had composed many gospel songs and choruses, some of which were to be featured during the revival campaign, and the *Globe Gazette* stated that Burroughs would conduct all of his own song services as well.

The meetings were entirely non-denominational and were open to the participation of other singers and musicians from Mason City, so long as their assistance would not conflict with their local organizations or churches. Guest artists from other various local churches were also invited to appear on the radio programs being broadcast out of the local radio station, which was KGLO Radio. Radio broadcasts of guest musicians were conducted each morning at 7:30 a.m. with the evening services that consisted of teaching and preaching beginning at 7:45 p.m. The favor of God rested strongly upon these services and people traveled frequently from great distances to be a part of the revival meetings, as there was a considerable hunger for evangelistic preaching in that day.

As attendance quickly grew, it became necessary to move the meetings from the restrictive size of the armory to a larger venue. A tent was erected at the corner of Pennsylvania Avenue and Second Street Northwest in Mason City, with services relocating there on Sunday August 1, 1937. The humble tent that helped serve as the beginning of Radio Chapel was not unlike any other tent of that day. Brown and unsightly, the canvas spanned a large portion of the ground and was tied and lashed to tent-posts and oak trees for support. The tent could seat several hundred people, and simple dirt paths led to its entrance. Cars and bicycles could be found parked at any given time on the grass surrounding the site during service times. If there was ever a Campmeeting feel to an event, this must have been what it felt like. It was quickly publicized throughout Mason City and the surrounding area that a large revival campaign was being conducted, and the continued success of the meetings only served to draw believers and non-believers alike to the continuous crusade.

Burroughs and Kathryn both preached frequently on the topics of the end times and the signs of the return of Jesus Christ, and these meetings were no exception. Burroughs used the relocation to the larger tent as an opportunity to preach the message "The Last Prophetical Sign before the Return of Christ." Members from several of the local churches were now regularly in attendance and were pleased with the revival meetings. Likewise, the morning messages that were broadcast over the local radio were so well received it was announced there would be an additional daily service in the tent, held at 3 p.m. solely for the purpose of lectures on the Book of Revelation.

In August 1937, Kathryn traveled to Milwaukee, Wisconsin, and held an evangelistic campaign that was met with outstanding success. She had been traveling more often and more extensively than ever before, many times finding capacity attendances of those coming to hear her messages. Following the conclusion of the

Milwaukee campaign, Kathryn planned to travel to Iowa to assist in the Mason City revival meetings, which were now in their sixth week. It was at this time that Burroughs, upon return from his own short evangelistic trip to Chicago, was presented with a petition signed by five hundred residents of Mason City and nearby counties. The petition stated:

> "We, the undersigned, citizens and people of, and in the vicinity of Mason City, Iowa, are interested in and feel a definite need of a continuous, independent, undenominational, evangelistic center for North Iowa; and hereby petition you to establish such a work, if this can be done consistent with the will of God."

In reporting the news of the petition, the *Globe Gazette* also stated that "nearly one hundred confessions of conversion have resulted from the Mason City revival campaign so far, and that hundreds have also come to the altar evidencing their desire to consecrate themselves to a Christian lifestyle." On Monday morning, August 30, 1937, the residents of North Iowa awoke to this article published in the Mason City *Globe Gazette*:

> Burroughs A. Waltrip, the Louisiana Pulpiteer, who has been conducting independent revival services under a tent at the corner of Pennsylvania Avenue and Second Street Northeast for the past six weeks, announced to his congregation Sunday evening that he will remain in Mason City to establish a permanent evangelistic center to be known as Radio Chapel.
>
> A petition signed by nearly 500 residents of Mason City and nearby communities was presented to the evangelist

recently asking that he establish a revival work for North Iowa. In his announcement the evangelist stated that he was not going to begin a new church in the ordinary acceptation of that word, but would carry on a continuous evangelistic campaign with services every night in the week, except Monday.

Mr. Waltrip's services have received the endorsement and cooperation of hundreds of North Iowa persons attending his meeting. One hundred and fourteen conversions have been recorded to date, the evangelist states.

Miss Kathryn Kuhlman, founder and director of one of the largest evangelistic works in the United States, located at Denver, Colorado, will be the guest speaker for the Tuesday evening service.

Miss Kuhlman has the reputation of being the nation's most successful young woman evangelist, Mr. Waltrip stated. She has just concluded a campaign in Milwaukee where she met with outstanding success. A capacity attendance is expected to hear her message. All the services are undenominational.

Keith Williams frequently expressed how exciting those times were. Electricity was in the air at the revival meetings. Those were the days of tent meetings, and such meetings were met with great success. People would travel near and far to come and hear the preacher. It was in this season that Burroughs and Kathryn found their callings in demand. America was hungry for good news. The horrible effects of the Depression still lingered on, and people were looking for hope and good news. Preachers like Burroughs and Kathryn delivered that good news.

In was in this environment of expectancy that Kathryn Kuhlman took the pulpit on Tuesday, August 31, 1937, and preached a message that Keith and Mary said, "Took your breath away." The sermon was titled "We Must Be Prepared."

We Must Be Prepared

Then shall the kingdom of heaven be likened unto ten virgins, which took their lamps, and went forth to meet the bridegroom. And five of them were wise, and five were foolish. They that were foolish took their lamps, and took no oil with them: But the wise took oil in their vessels with their lamps. While the bridegroom tarried, they all slumbered and slept. And at midnight there was a cry made, Behold, the bridegroom cometh; go ye out to meet him. Then all those virgins arose, and trimmed their lamps. And the foolish said unto the wise, Give us of your oil; for our lamps are gone out. But the wise answered, saying, Not so; lest there be not enough for us and you: but go ye rather to them that sell, and buy for yourselves. And while they went to buy, the bridegroom came; and they that were ready went in with him to the marriage: and the door was shut. Afterward came also the other virgins, saying, Lord, Lord, open to us. But he answered and said, Verily I say unto you, I know you not. Watch therefore, for ye know neither the day nor the hour wherein the Son

of man cometh. For the kingdom of heaven is as a man travelling into a far country, who called his own servants, and delivered unto them his goods.

Matthew 25:1–14 (KJV)

All the world over, men have always regarded marriage as one of life's happiest events, and perhaps they always will. The Bible, in general, and our Lord in particular, have much to say of marriage. Jesus showed a very remarkable interest in marriage. He performed His first miracle on the occasion of a wedding celebration. Once He told a parable that was based on the theme of marriage when He spoke of the man who appeared at the wedding feast without the right kind of a garment.

Jesus also liked to speak of Himself as a Bridegroom and all those who believed in Him as His beloved bride. The parable related in the text that I just read to you is likewise based on this general theme. This parable is to teach us two particular truths: Firstly, the truth that the Bridegroom is coming, and secondly, the truth that we should be ready to greet Him when He comes.

Marriage customs were somewhat different in Palestine from those we observe in our own country today. In our Lord's time and native land, it was customary for the groom to go with his attendants to the home of the bride to get her and take her home with him. The bride and her friends, or bridesmaids, would wait for his coming, and when they received the notice that the groom was approaching, the bridesmaids would go out to meet him. Then, with song and jubilation, they brought him to the home of the bride.

While our text does not linger for long on this particular truth, that the bridegroom comes to get the bride, it is yet a truth that the parable teaches and one of the truly important truths of the Bible. Just as this bridegroom went to the home of his bride to get her, Jesus would have us understand, as well, that He as the Heavenly Bridegroom is going to come and get His bride, so that they may be with Him in His home above.

Jesus is going to come again. He will make His appearance at a time whereof we know not. He will come in all His Heavenly glory and splendor attended by a vast company of Heavenly hosts. Then, when He comes, all men of all time will stand before Him.

But, the principal point of our parable is to teach us that we should be ready when Jesus comes. Our text tells us of the bridesmaids who were sitting with the bride and who intended to go out and meet the bridegroom when he came. It was the groom, in those days, who might come late. In our day, the situation is changed. If we are kept waiting in the church, it is usually because the bride is late. However in those days if anyone was late, it was the groom.

In this instance, with the groom delayed apparently for some time, with the result that the hour grew late, the bride and the bridesmaids fell asleep. At last, the bride and her bridesmaids were informed that the groom was approaching. At once there was a great commotion about going out and meeting him. But, because more time had elapsed than they had counted on, some of the bridesmaids were not in a position to go. They had brought their lamps, but such oil had already been used up. Therefore, they were not prepared when the moment came in which they should go forth.

You and I all know enough about life to realize how true and how applicable this is to men in general. We all know foolish virgins, that is to say, foolish people who cannot and will not think far enough to prepare themselves for whatever tomorrow might bring forth.

So, we say to the young that youth is the time of preparation. You must study. You must learn something. If you don't learn and study, you will not be ready when opportunity knocks. But say what you will, some are so foolish that they will not give heed.

What is true of studies and preparation is true of other aspects of life. It applies to health. Some people spend their health as though they did not expect to live tomorrow. This applies to the economy. Some just cannot think of tomorrow. What they have today, they must get rid of.

My friends, if men are improvident concerning their bodily needs, this is yet more true and more common when applied to their spiritual needs. The Bible plainly teaches that Jesus is coming again to judge the world in righteousness. The Bible plainly teaches that men must eventually stand before their Heavenly Judge. And yet, men go on living without a thought of tomorrow. They make no preparation to meet the Bridegroom. He is coming. But they are not thinking of when He might come.

And I will say this; the danger of such neglect is especially great in a church such as ours. We can get so busy with business or professional responsibilities that we forget everything else, while these things loom so large ahead of us. We therefore fail to give due consideration to the soul.

What is true of the male members is true also of the female members of our church, for she can so easily spend all her time and thought on things other than spiritual.

Nothing can be more tragic than the failure to prepare. When the bridegroom finally came, the girls who had brought no additional oil had none for their lamps, and therefore could not go out to meet him.

They asked the wise virgins to share their supply of oil with them, but they said, "No, we can't do that. If you want oil, you must go to the merchants and buy some." Perhaps, it will suggest itself to you that the wise virgins were rather selfish and that they should have shared their oil.

Well, had it been a matter of oil that might have been done, but the oil in the parable represents something other than oil. You know that the person who studies and prepares himself for some task in life cannot go to an unprepared person at whose door opportunity may knock and say to him, "Take what I have learned and use it." He can't do that. You may be able to share your oil, but you can't share your preparation.

When the Heavenly Bridegroom comes, they who have faith and have lived a Christian life cannot share their faith and give half of it to those who made no preparation. They, who then are not prepared, cannot go out to meet the Bridegroom. And once the groom has entered the bride's house, the door is shut.

When opportunity knocks at your door, you must be prepared to open the door and greet it. It is equally true that when the Heavenly Bridegroom comes, you are either prepared or you are shut out.

If you do not give heed to this warning of our Lord's people today, you shut the door against yourself. This opportunity can never come back. If a year from now or so it should be my privilege to speak on the same message, it will not be the same opportunity. You will have lost at least one year of spiritual peace and happiness.

But, this also speaks to those who know Christ and have made preparation for His coming. We know that this preparation cannot be made today, yet be allowed to go unheeded tomorrow.

If you have company coming and you cleaned your home all spic and span but they don't come and don't come, your house gets dirty again and the dust settles around again. So it is with our spiritual houses. We have prepared, but the Lord has not come. Therefore we have gotten careless. The dust of worldliness has crept in unnoticed. The trash of unconcern has littered up the front steps. The playthings of pleasure have scattered themselves all over the floor of our homes, and, if Jesus were to come, we would not be prepared. The windows of our hearts are not shining brightly. Our lights are not burning brightly.

There is a story told of a rich woman who went to Heaven and went down several streets before finally coming to her meager home. She was surprised. The angel said, "That's the best we could do with what you sent up."

Finally, whether it be today or whether it be tomorrow, whether we close our eyes in the sleep of death and be summoned hence in that manner, or whether in the twinkling of an eye the heavens should burst with glory and the King and Bridegroom should make His appearance, let us be ready. Let us not be without oil, but may the torch of faith be burning brightly.

May God, in His infinite mercy, grant that each one of us will take this blessed truth to heart, so that we may not be as the foolish virgins, but as the wise virgins, prepared to greet the Bridegroom when He comes.

Just because the preaching had ended did not mean the service was over. Many times the dirt and sawdust altar became flooded with people. "We would stay and pray with anyone who wanted prayer," Keith said. "People really liked that kind of preaching and it really hit their hearts, so we would just spend time praying and talking with them, sometimes up until midnight." Kathryn, of course, was wholeheartedly received and celebrated by her hearers.

Chapter Three

KATHRYN THE EVANGELIST

Preach the word; be instant in season, out of season; reprove, rebuke, exhort with all longsuffering and doctrine.

2 Timothy 4:2 (KJV)

"*Miss Kathryn Kuhlman, founder and director of one of the largest evangelistic works in the United States, located at Denver, Colorado, will be the guest speaker for the upcoming revival campaign.*" These were the words emblazed upon handbills, posters, and newspaper ads that introduced and invited the masses to come and hear Kathryn speak. By August 1937, she had established herself as one of the nation's most successful and sought after young woman evangelists. Kathryn had entered into a season of both promotion and favor, gaining the respect and admiration of believers and non-believers alike. She also garnered great support from pastors and churches everywhere as she experienced a steadily growing demand for her unique style of ministry. Kathryn's distinctive approach to ministry influenced her attire, her speaking, and her ministry mannerisms. The platform was her place of influence, where the preacher in her was set free.

Both Keith and Mary Williams had previously seen Kathryn preach at other revival campaigns in the region before eventually becoming her assistants at Radio Chapel. These campaigns were extremely popular in the 1930's and very often became the focal point of a town's interest while being conducted. It wasn't unusual to see businesses and shops close early so that families could attend the local revival meetings. Oftentimes, taverns and other alcoholic establishments as well as gambling houses would see their revenues plunge due to the meetings, which could easily continue three weeks or more. Revival meetings, many times held in tents, were a staple of the day and had the potential to impact an entire region.

"You know, when you look way, way back," Mary told me, "Keith and I were very young when we started out in revival meetings. I think it was those revival meetings we were in during those years that made a difference. I've never seen it like it was during those times. I've never seen it again like it was back then when the altar couldn't handle all the people. You don't see that anymore. Isn't that true? We don't see this today because people are kind of dulled by the world. We are living in the Laodicean age, aren't we?"

There was an atmosphere of expectation in those tent meetings. People came with anticipation in their hearts and a readiness to participate. The old canvas "tabernacles" as they were called, hastily erected on the outskirts of town, quickly became a destination for people far and near. There was a Campmeeting aura that people loved, and the sawdust floor, wooden benches, and light bulbs strung on electrical cords only served to further the sensation. Many times the platform would be constructed for the event by volunteer laborers building with wood donated from local lumber stores.

THE PLATFORM

The platform was Kathryn's wheelhouse. It was here that she came alive. Everything about her fit the role of a modern-day evangelist. Her passion and eloquence would bless the crowds immensely on a continual basis. And her attire reflected her role as well. "She wore a long, white gown while preaching," Keith reflected. "She wore the gown because it made her feel more religious and spiritual." Mary continued, "She was on high platforms a lot and, of course, you know she couldn't stand still," she said with a smile. "She was there and there and there, back and forth," Mary added, gesturing with her hands.

Most notable to Keith was the fact that Kathryn was so gentle in the delivery of her messages. It was disarming, that same gentleness, as many times her messages dealt with serious Biblical topics such as the dangers of sin, the reality of Heaven and Hell, and the tragedy of rejecting Jesus Christ. "There really isn't a lot known about those early years of Kathryn Kuhlman's ministry," Keith said, as he continued to reflect on Kathryn's fledgling years. "But she really was timid and sensitive and sweet. And she never criticized." Mary built on Keith's words, "Yes, she was very timid, but she wouldn't show it if she was near you. Do you know what I mean? She was a sweetheart. And when she would get up on the platform, she wasn't timid there! That's when her gift took over."

In seven years of intensive work, Kathryn had risen from the ranks of an unknown preacher to the place of the most sought after young woman evangelist of her day. This was especially amazing, considering the fact that Kathryn had no special ministerial training and as a child felt led of the Lord to enter the evangelistic field. Now in her mid-twenties, she had already held meetings in the leading Gospel centers of the country and was drawing tens of thousands to her campaigns by her unusual style of preaching and anointed messages. In 1937 alone, Kathryn's campaigns were met with marvelous success in the cities of Milwaukee, Detroit, Chicago, Minneapolis, Peoria, Denver, and Waterloo. Capacity attendances turned out for each event, and many times the meetings were extended well out beyond the scheduled completion date.

After holding a number of independent meetings, Kathryn eventually held a meeting in Denver, Colorado. These extended meetings proved so stirring and successful that she was asked to build an independent non-denominational Gospel work there. It was at her church in Denver where she oversaw what was considered to be one of the finest young person's ministries in the nation. Keith observed, "She talked a lot about her church in Colorado from the platform. She really did."

Newspapers, when publishing a story regarding an upcoming revival campaign, routinely wrote that Kathryn had a most unusual and pleasant platform personality. That personality, coupled with her ability as a preacher, easily made her the greatest female preacher in America.

Assisting Kathryn in many of her meetings at Radio Chapel was Miss Helen Gulliford and Mr. Harry D. Clarke. Miss Gulliford was an accomplished pianist and the song composer at Denver Revival Tabernacle and was considered one of America's finest Gospel pianists. Helen studied in Los Angeles and New York City, playing before audiences numbering more than 10,000 on a number of occasions. She had previously worked alongside Kathryn in revival campaigns for the past seven years. Helen was also the composer of a number of Gospel songs, many of which were featured in Kathryn's campaigns. Harry D. Clarke was the founder and director of Clarke's Tabernacle in Waterloo, Iowa, and oversaw much of the choir work and congregational singing during Kathryn's campaigns. Harry was a song leader for William "Billy" Sunday, another noted evangelist of that day. As a result of his having ministered with Billy Sunday, Harry was well known throughout the country for his capabilities as both a song leader and an evangelist.

Thousands of souls were won to the Lord as a result of Kathryn's meetings. Being thoroughly versed in the Bible, she had no problem in either composing or preaching her most memorable sermons. As an evangelist of that era, Kathryn customarily ministered on a variety of topics, such as the second coming of Jesus Christ, the Great Tribulation, and the church in the last days. "The Last Judgment" was a favorite message of hers and therefore was preached in a number of her regional crusades.

The Last Judgment

And I saw an angel come down from heaven, having the key of the bottomless pit and a great chain in his hand. And he laid hold on the dragon, that old serpent, which is the Devil, and Satan, and bound him a thousand years, And cast him into the bottomless pit, and shut him up, and set a seal upon him, that he should deceive the nations no more, till the thousand years should be fulfilled: and after that he must be loosed a little season.

Revelation 20:1-3 (KJV)

When Christ returns to the earth, many important things will take place. He will leave Heaven with the saints, riding upon a white horse, and come to the battle of Armageddon. He will quickly gain victory in this battle because of the sword that proceeds out of His mouth. The beast, Antichrist, and false prophet who will bring together the armies of the earth, will be captured and cast alive into a lake of fire, burning with brimstone. After a thousand years, they are still found in that place of suffering.

After the battle of Armageddon comes a great supper. It is the supper of the flesh-eating birds. These fowls of the air are called together by the angel who stands in the sun. They come to devour the flesh of kings and captains and mighty men, and of all men great and small who are destroyed in the battle of Armageddon. Revelation 19 closes with this notation:

And the remnant were slain with the sword of him that sat upon the horse, which sword proceeded out of his mouth: and all the fowls were filled with their flesh.

Revelation 19:21 (KJV)

We now come to a consideration of the last three years of Revelation chapter 20 that tells us of the chaining of Satan. Satan is not bound now, but he will be.

And he laid hold on the dragon, that old serpent, which is the Devil, and Satan, and bound him a thousand years.

Revelation 20:2 (KJV)

After Satan was cast out of Heaven, he made the scene of his action on the earth and in the air above the earth. In the Garden of Eden, he caused the first downfall of man. Throughout the Old Testament, we find that he caused the people of God to forsake the Lord and engage in doubtful practices. In the New Testament days, Satan was still busy. He tempted the Lord. He used Judas Iscariot. In the days following the New Testament, Satan is still busy. Christians have always had a battle with him. Some of the Christians have been destroyed by him. Churches have been torn asunder by his onslaughts. Nations have disappeared who allowed his power to be exercised.

But one of these days, he will be bound. And, after the binding of Satan, the earth will begin to improve. The earth will begin to blossom like a garden when he is no longer here to damn and destroy. Satan is going to be bound like a common criminal and cast into the bottomless pit. The world will no longer be his arena. He will be cast out of the earth.

Friends, before world conditions can improve, the influence of Satan must be stopped. As long as he is the prince of the power of the air and the god of this world, there will be sin and darkness. Thank God, Satan is going to be bound. Following the binding of Satan, the curse that is upon the earth will be lifted! Remember what happened in Genesis:

And unto Adam he said, Because thou hast hearkened unto the voice of thy wife, and hast eaten of the tree, of which I commanded thee, saying, Thou shalt not eat of it: cursed is the ground for thy sake; in sorrow shalt thou eat of it all the days of thy life; Thorns also and thistles shall it bring forth to thee; and thou shalt eat the herb of the field.

Genesis 3:17-18 (KJV)

But with the binding of Satan, the curse of Genesis will be lifted and the earth will be blessed of God. The earth will blossom as a rose when Jesus establishes His Kingdom upon the earth.

And I saw an angel come down from heaven, having the key of the bottomless pit and a great chain in his hand. And he laid hold on the dragon, that old serpent, which is the Devil, and Satan, and bound him a thousand years, And cast him into the bottomless pit, and shut him up, and set a seal upon him, that he should deceive the nations no more, till the thousand years should be

fulfilled: and after that he must be loosed a little season. And I saw thrones, and they sat upon them, and judgment was given unto them: and I saw the souls of them that were beheaded for the witness of Jesus, and for the word of God, and which had not worshipped the beast, neither his image, neither had received his mark upon their foreheads, or in their hands; and they lived and reigned with Christ a thousand years. But the rest of the dead lived not again until the thousand years were finished. This is the first resurrection. Blessed and holy is he that hath part in the first resurrection: on such the second death hath no power, but they shall be priests of God and of Christ, and shall reign with him a thousand years.

Revelation 20:1-6 (KJV)

And Christ will rule with His Saints! They lived and reigned with Christ one thousand years. The length of this reign is mentioned six times.

Now, following these tremendous events given in the first ten verses of Revelation chapter 20, we have the account of the last judgment. This is the final judgment. The great white throne judgment is the final scene before the new Heaven and the new Earth. Where will it take place? When will it take place? What will be the results? Who will be there? What does it mean to be thrown into the lake of fire? Let's get Scripture for all of this.

And I saw a great white throne, and him that sat on it, from whose face the earth and the heaven fled away; and there was found no place for them. And I saw the dead, small and great, stand before God; and the books were opened: and another book was opened, which is the book of life: and the dead were judged out of those things which were written in the books, according to their works. And the sea gave up the dead which were in it; and death and hell delivered up the dead which were in them: and they were judged every man according to their works. And death and hell were cast into the lake of fire. This is the second death. And whosoever was not found written in the book of life was cast into the lake of fire.

Revelation 20:11-15 (KJV)

It is a great white throne, because the lost of the earth will stand before the Lord. It is a white throne, for it reveals the holiness and purity of God. The One who sits upon the throne will be Christ, for He said:

For the Father judgeth no man, but hath committed all judgment unto the Son: That all men should honour the Son, even as they honour the Father. He that hono-ureth not the Son honoureth not the Father which hath sent him.

John 5:22-23 (KJV)

And remember, I'm telling you as true as God is in Heaven, if you don't change and give your heart to Christ, you'll stand before the Lord Jesus Christ at the great white throne judgment. The Holy Spirit will be there to witness against you. You'll remember when He spoke to you, when He convicted you, when He touched you and when you said,

"Yes, I ought to do it. I know it's the thing to do." But, you didn't do it.

You will remember your dying mother who pled for the family to be ready. You'll remember your father when he was sick. But, the next day, you were back in the world and trying to forget your feelings that the Holy Spirit put into your heart. You will remember. You will remember the time you said, "I sure had a wonderful mother," and, as you walked away from the grave and back to your car, you felt as if you left something behind. That was the Holy Spirit.

Oh, if you had only yielded. If you had bowed your head and your heart. If you had carried through with your better judgment, the whole thing would have been settled. But now, at the white throne judgment, you must stand and face the Lord Jesus Christ, who died for you. You will see His hands, His feet, and His gashed side. But now, it's too late. Too late. You were almost persuaded—almost—but now lost. This is the judgment of the lost dead. The Word teaches plainly the fact of two resurrections:

And many of them that sleep in the dust of the earth shall awake, some to everlasting life, and some to shame and everlasting contempt.

Daniel 12:2 (KJV)

So, at the first coming of Christ, the saved will be resurrected, and at the time of the great white throne judgment, the wicked dead shall be resurrected.

And the sea gave up the dead which were in it; and death and hell delivered up the dead which were in them: and they were judged every man according to their works.

Revelation 20:13 (KJV)

This is the resurrection of the unsaved. This is the time when the graves will give up the bodies of the lost and Hades will surrender the spirits and souls of the lost. They will be reunited and will be brought to stand before the judgment of God.

And I saw the dead, small and great, stand before God; and the books were opened: and another book was opened, which is the book of life: and the dead were judged out of those things which were written in the books, according to their works.

Revelation 20:12 (KJV)

The record books will be there. Every man's sins will be plainly written down. Every man will be judged out of the record. All sins will be brought to light. The young, the middle-aged, and the old will see their lives pass before them. Secret sins will be brought to light. There are things that you have done which no one knows about but God. He has it all written down. If you die without Christ, you will face it. God's records are exact. He makes no mistakes. Sins never committed openly will also be brought to light. John says:

Whosoever hateth his brother is a murderer: and ye know that no murderer hath eternal life abiding in him.

1 John 3:15 (KJV)

Yes, all sins will be brought to light. But the greatest sin will be that of the rejection of Jesus Christ. There is no sin so terrible as refusing the loving Savior.

We notice now that another book was opened, which is the Book of Life. If this is the judgment of the unsaved, then why should the Book of Life be present? It is there as a record against the lost. Even in the last judgment there will doubtless be men who will insist that they are good and deserve Heaven. They will search through the Book of Life and, with their name missing, they will be condemned. Remember, unsaved friends, you will have to face your record. Nothing will be omitted. The outcome of this judgment is this:

And death and hell were cast into the lake of fire. This is the second death. And whosoever was not found written in the book of life was cast into the lake of fire.

Revelation 20:14-15 (KJV)

This is a verse of finality. This is the future certainty for the Christ rejecter. There is no escaping from Hell for the man who has heard and refused to accept Christ.

Chapter Four

THE HOUSE THAT GOD BUILT

**For every house is built by someone, but the builder of
all things is God.**

Hebrews 3:4 (NASB)

The first week of September 1937 brought with it a fundraising campaign for the construction of Radio Chapel. The tent was now full every night and people either sat or stood to hear the description of what was planned. They visualized a non-denominational community tabernacle, which would be called Radio Chapel, and would be unique among all the world's churches of worship. Upon the launch of the fundraising campaign at a Sunday evening service, a $1,000 pledge and three $500 pledges were made, in addition to other smaller pledges. Construction of the shell of the main auditorium was scheduled to begin in ninety days. A deal was made with the Masonic Lodge for the purchase of the land upon which the tent was presently erected, making it possible to build Radio Chapel

45

on the site. The enthusiasm was becoming contagious amongst all who attended the ongoing services.

Burroughs, in describing the planned facility, told his listeners the building would be, "as smart as tomorrow's sunrise." Radio Chapel was designed to be air-conditioned throughout and would be built without a single window, according to plans. The lighting would be indirect, coupled with inspiring lighting effects. In a departure from what was traditionally practiced, there were to be no hymnals. When music would be played from the electric organ, the words of that particular hymn would be projected onto a screen far above the altar. Another interesting feature was to be a hydraulically controlled disappearing pulpit that could be lowered into the floor and raised again at the touch of a button. Additionally, plans were shared for the inclusion of the technology needed to conduct future radio broadcasts from the facility. Truly, this was to be a one-of-a-kind church.

Keith Williams shared that Kathryn travelled back and forth frequently between Mason City and her church in Denver, Colorado. She assisted in vision development and fundraising for Radio Chapel while at the same time overseeing her large congregation at the Denver Revival Tabernacle. It wasn't unusual to see a number of Kathryn's friends and leaders from her Denver work travelling with her and assisting her with her meetings and crusades in other states. Kathryn had a magnetism about her that would draw people to her side. She was a lover of God and therefore a lover of people, always believing the best of both. Mary conveyed that Kathryn routinely shared of her great love and admiration for the congregation of Denver Revival Tabernacle. "They allowed me to be the preacher that I am today," she would say.

An Invitation

The following letter was sent out from Radio Chapel to the residents and businesses of North Iowa in the early fall of 1937. At that time, the operational staff consisted of Burroughs Waltrip, Kathryn Kuhlman, and Keith Williams. The following letter was personally signed by Burroughs A. Waltrip on behalf of Radio Chapel's ministry team:

> Hello Everybody! Will you give a few minutes to the Lord? Please read the enclosed "word picture" of Radio Chapel, "The Most Unique Church in the World," which we are building in Mason City for North Iowa. Thanks a lot for the courtesy of your time and thought. The Lord bless you good.

Radio Chapel: The Most Unique Church in the World

> In Hebrews 8:5, Moses was admonished of God when he was about to build the tabernacle; "For, see, saith He (God), that thou make all things according to the pattern showed to thee in the mount." How wonderful to know what God wants done and how!
>
> Paul, before King Agrippa, told of the wonderful vision he saw on the Damascus road and testified with a flowing heart in Acts 26:19, "Whereupon, O King Agrippa, I was not disobedient unto the heavenly vision." How wonderful to do what God wants done, as He wants it done!

THE GREAT NEED OF MAKING OLD TRUTHS VIBRANT

Jesus, in Luke 16:8, made a very startling statement that is certainly applicable to the hour in which we live: "The children of this world are in their generation wiser than the children of light." Many manufacturers in recent years have learned that by redesigning the color and coverings of their packages, they have been enabled to double or more the sales of their products without making any change in the product itself. There certainly needs to be no change in the Gospel message. It is God's eternal Truth and He particularly warns us against adding to or taking from it, but the methods that are being used for the presentation of the Gospel are outmoded and are failing.

All too often, the place of worship and the manner of the service presentation are a bore rather than an inspiration and soul satisfaction. That is not only true concerning the young people, but the older folks as well. Christianity will fairly sparkle if allowed to do so. Nothing in the universe is so beautiful, so colorful, and so attractive as the real Gospel of Jesus Christ. It isn't the Gospel that is failing, it is the way we are presenting it, and yet our services are not necessarily Scriptural. They are traditional. Somebody needs to lead us out of the rut as Luther did in his day, Wesley in his, and Simpson in his.

Paul, in writing to the people in 1 Corinthians 9:2, made the statement, "I am made all things to all men, that I might by all means save some." I believe that Paul would have sanctioned this statement, "If by changing our plans of worship and our manner and mode of services, we can win more souls to Jesus Christ—then it is a tragedy not to do so." Let us make the old truths vibrant!

A Cherished Vision of Many Years

It has been a cherished vision of my heart to swing clear of rutted tradition; to forget all about the ordinary church precedence, and tackle the matter of preaching Jesus Christ; designing the place of worship and manner and conduct of services in a fresh and vigorous way, and if possible, from a new perspective, I have longed to make God's house and His work the bright and glorious center of all community interests. I have wanted to give the Gospel a real chance at the hearts of all the people, not only the down-and-outers, but also the up-and-outers. All of us need the Gospel.

The Type of Program to Be Conducted

The great need of the hour in this section, as in others, is for a dynamic evangelistic program, having for its purpose the winning of souls and the establishment of their hearts in sound Christian truths. Radio Chapel will conduct such a program and will be entirely undenominational and with absolutely no membership. It will be free of organizational domination. Services will be held every night in the year (except Monday) and on Sunday afternoons. The early New Testament Church broke bread daily and was commanded not to forsake the assembling of their selves together.

And they, continuing daily with one accord in the temple, and breaking bread from house to house, did eat their meat with gladness and singleness of heart.

Acts 2:46 (KJV)

And daily in the temple, and in every house, they ceased not to teach and preach Jesus Christ.

Acts 5:42 (KJV)

Not forsaking the assembling of ourselves together, as the manner of some is; but exhorting one another: and so much the more, as ye see the day approaching.

Hebrews 10:25 (KJV)

It will be our pleasure to present to the Radio Chapel congregation the nation's greatest preachers, evangelists, and Bible teachers as our guests. The musical features will include the young people's chorus, electric organ, grand piano, sacred orchestra, and special music.

There will be no Sunday School but in its stead, we will conduct the most unusual children's organization about which we know. It will be a children's church that will meet every Saturday morning at 10 o'clock. The children themselves will take a large part and will actually "play church." We will work with the child preacher of the week and help him in the presentation of a ten-minute sermonette. He will be aided by a pianist and song leader. Other children will lead in prayer and offer testimonies. It may look like play to their fathers and mothers, but these children will never in the world get away from the truths that they themselves have learned to set forth.

The young people's work may well nigh be called the heart of the Radio Chapel program. They will make up the body of the choir and take part on Gospel teams that will carry the Message to the smaller churches over this section where doors are opened to it. A special service will be conducted by and for them each Sunday evening before the evening service.

There will be no Ladies' Aid, but there will be a definite women's work. The women will meet one day a week for a devotional program, season of prayer, and then will spend some hours in the preparation of baby linens, assorting out and repairing of used clothing and any other ministry that may come to their hands for the benefit of the poor who attend Radio Chapel or who are administered to by the Chapel.

The men's fellowship will provide an undenominational men's meeting at least once a quarter when the men who are interested in the promotion of the work of Radio Chapel may meet, discuss its possibilities and problems and enjoy an evening of congenial fellowship with other like-hearted men.

One of my dreams which must come true one of these days soon is that of a faith Bible school, where young men and young women may receive the finest type of Bible training and ministerial instruction, regardless of their ability to pay. Plans are now being formed and will likely be put into effect within the next twelve months for the establishment of such a school in Mason City.

The radio ministry of Radio Chapel will, of course, be an outstanding feature. The completed Chapel will have its own studio from which inspirational broadcasts will come twice daily, 7:30 a.m. and 10:15 p.m. There will be, insofar as is practicable, a registration of all radio listeners who will be visited twice or more often during the year by workers from Radio Chapel.

It will further be the pleasure of the evangelistic staff of Radio Chapel to cooperate in the fullest measure with any and all churches regardless of size or strength in the evangelistic programs, since our solo aim is to bring about an outspread revival in this section.

A constant prayer program will be enacted, with prayer teams constantly waiting on the Lord for the Radio Chapel work, as well as the individual requests that are being sent for in prayer.

THE RADIO CHAPEL BUILDING

You will be interested in the Radio Chapel itself. We are determined to make it "as smart as tomorrow's sunrise." Although it will not be highly expensive, it will be entirely original and different. The basement will house the young people's auditorium, the prayer room, the heating plant, men's and women's lounges, and restrooms. On the main floor, there will be the Chapel offices and radio studio, which will broadcast by remote control over KGLO. The Chapel auditorium itself, when completed, will seat 1,000 persons. It will measure 60 by 100 foot. Beautiful lighting effects will be made possible by a large neon cross in the *ceiling and indirect lighting from all sides. Indirect lighting windows are an innovation in church architecture, as will be also the lighted Scriptural mottoes, which will be controlled by rheostat.*

The auditorium and all parts of the building will be air-conditioned, and kept at a healthful temperature every hour of the day and night. The color scheme to be carried out will be silver, which is a scriptural type of redemption and dark blue that is a type of God's righteousness. The carpet runner and drapes will all be in harmony with this color scheme. The seats will be opera chairs of the latest design in mahogany and silver leatherette.

The Radio Chapel platform will be the "voice box" type. The seating arrangement on the platform for the choir will be most unique. It will be a broken aisle arrangement that will enable every seat to stand out from all the rest. The pulpit will be the only one of its kind in the world, as far as we know. During the preliminary services, it will be entirely out of sight, but when we are ready for the sermon, a button pushed will cause the pulpit to rise from the front of the platform.

There will be no song books used in the finished Radio Chapel, but a song screen above the song leader's head will have placed upon it the verse of the songs in use. The baptistery will be located at the rear of the platform on a raised platform and will be so constructed that water will run through it continuously and the scene of the River Jordan beautifully discernable in the background. A heavy curtain on an electric track will shield the choir until it is in place and ready for the song service. As the curtain moves back at the touch of a button, the rheostat-controlled lights come up and the service begins. An altar will run the entire width of the auditorium immediately in front of the platform.

The building will be constructed by units so as to enable us to pay for most of it as construction proceeds, thus preventing the discouraging hindrance of old obligations. The first unit to be constructed will be the shell of the auditorium proper. Work on this part of the building is to be started by the middle of September.

THE LOCATION OF RADIO CHAPEL

Some months ago I was praying in the early morning. The burden of Mason City was laid on my heart, even though I knew nothing of the place. I had never been here. I had never had correspondence from here and knew no one who lived here. It appeared impossible at the time for me to come because of heavy bookings for revival campaigns, but after much prayer, the Lord worked it out so that I might obey the call that I felt in my heart. After the meetings had been in progress for six weeks, a petition was presented with signatures of nearly 500 residents of Mason City and North Iowa requesting that I establish a permanent revival center here. During these weeks also, I have caught the vision of this great North Iowa "Harvest Field" and I have felt that God will give a mighty gathering of souls to the man who has the anointing and can feel the burden for them.

The kind of work that God wants here, the kind that I have had on my heart for years, will of necessity occupy a place that will gain the respect of the community as well as be a convenience for the community. I have felt that we must have one of the most attractive lots in the city. I laid this fleece before the Lord: If He would give me a certain quarter block that I was praying about, I would feel in my heart that He would give me the beautiful Radio Chapel complete. He did make it possible for us to get that lot. We are now holding a revival campaign on it at the corner of Pennsylvania Avenue and Second Street Northeast.

This Is Not an Idle Dream

It is my earnest desire to capture the public imagination for Jesus Christ. It is my hope to give Northern Iowa a thrillingly different place to find the Lord; to make a striking appeal to the young people of all this section; to establish a spiritual center, as well as an outstanding tourist attraction. Radio Chapel will be all this and more, "The Most Unique Church in the World." This is not an idle dream. Every feature of the program is spiritually sound, and every part of the building feature is architecturally feasible.

Can you catch the vision? And will you be obedient to it? Will you be my partner in this glorious adventure with the Lord in these last days? Will you make a thrilling sacrifice with me?

There is a card for your convenience enclosed. Fill it in and put it in the enclosed envelope and send it to me by return mail, or if you prefer, enclose your check. I am sure you will want to have your part in North Iowa's great revival

center. Thanks from the bottom of my heart!—Burroughs A.
Waltrip

In reality, Radio Chapel was shaping up to be one of the nation's first seeker-sensitive, media-driven ministries. Although projection screens, disappearing pulpits, and indirect lighting are common in America today, these things were unheard of in Kathryn Kuhlman's day.

By mid-September, the revival tent had been moved to the extreme northeast corner of the lot that had been recently purchased for the location of the new Radio Chapel, so that daily services could continue. Construction was to begin soon on the first unit of the facility, which was to be the shell of the main auditorium. The local newspaper reported that "at the close of service on Tuesday, September 14, 1937, the first spade full of dirt would be turned for the foundation at a groundbreaking service and ceremony." More than $2,300 had been already pledged toward the construction of Radio Chapel. The vision had been cast and the people were responding with their time, treasure, and talents.

Both the purpose and the architecture embodied in the building were a sharp departure from the norm. Radio Chapel was to be "the most unique church in the world," and was described to people as the natural outgrowth of the independent revival campaign that began in July 1937, an outreach that was still ongoing. Burroughs, in an interview with the *Globe Gazette* published on Tuesday, October 26, 1937, stated:

"I hope to make it definitely understood that there is emphatically no connection between Radio Chapel and any other work of any nature anywhere," added Mr. Waltrip. "There is no superior governing body. All authority is centered in the local work. It is independent in the purest meaning of the word.

"It is also my earnest desire to have the people understand that Radio Chapel is entirely undenominational. It makes absolutely no difference to me which church the people join. There is nothing at Radio Chapel for them to join but the Lord. There is now and there will be no membership. The sole purpose of the work is Bible evangelism.

"Although Radio Chapel will be conducted under the laws of Iowa governing a non-profit benevolent work, a most accurate set of books is being kept and subject to audit at regular intervals. Even though there is no governing board, every restriction possible for the secretary of the work is being enacted in the Chapel business conduct.

"Many innovations in church architecture will appear in the interior construction of the building. It will be as nearly acoustically perfect as possible. It will be air-conditioned the year round.

"Services will be conducted every night in the year, except Mondays, and on Sunday afternoons. Many of the nation's greatest preachers will be guest speakers at the Chapel.

"No personal or promiscuous solicitation of funds will be made by any group of persons. All contributions to the

*construction of the building and the support of the program
must be voluntary."*

The newspaper interview ended with Burroughs commenting, "I
am making Mason City my home and permanent headquarters, and
hope to prove a help in every possible way in advancing the moral
and spiritual interests of all the people of every church affiliation as
well as non-church members."

By mid-fall, Keith and Mary Williams had officially been added
to the Radio Chapel staff, as well as Ralph Geer as the Chapel
pianist. Ralph was a regional music director who had served at a
number of area churches. Revival broadcasts continued to be presented over KGLO radio every morning at 7:30 a.m., and plans were
being finalized to eventually broadcast all services from the soon to
be constructed Chapel.

Kathryn was busy commuting between her churches in Mason
City and Denver. In addition to her growing responsibilities, she
also continued to hold wildly successful crusades whenever possible. Her preaching schedule was always full. It was evident that
Kathryn struck a chord with her audience wherever she traveled.
She was loved and accepted by all who heard her. Mary shared that
Kathryn was always at Radio Chapel, even more so than her church
in Denver at times. She said that Kathryn used to travel back and
forth between Iowa and Colorado, eventually deciding to base her
ministry out of Mason City while at the same time overseeing the
church in Denver. This obviously resulted in the people in Denver
growing increasingly discouraged without Kathryn there with them.

"She was able to do all of this, though, because Kathryn was a great leader," Mary added.

By November 1937, construction on the new Radio Chapel was in full swing. Burroughs instituted a series of fasts while believing for the remaining money to come in that was needed for the completion of the first phase of the building. The amount of money that the Radio Chapel staff was believing God for in that day was quite large—$5,000 was needed in November with another $10,000 the following February. Once again, Burroughs utilized the newspaper and radio to explain his methods.

In the Thursday, November 4, 1937, edition of the *Globe Gazette*, Burroughs explained the necessity of being "led to fast" while trusting God for finances. Excerpts from that article read,

> *Pulpiteer says he won't eat until $5,000 is raised for chapel. Burroughs A. Waltrip, Louisiana pulpiteer, will continue a period of prayer and fasting, started last Sunday, until a sum of not less than $5,000 is raised for the completion of the first unit of the Radio Chapel, which is under construction at Pennsylvania Avenue and Second Street Northeast, according to Keith Williams, Mr. Waltrip's assistant.*
>
> *"The work and program of Radio Chapel was begun and will always be conducted entirely by faith. It has no membership and so could put on no membership drive even though we cared to, which we do not. The entire amount needed for finishing the building, as we believe the Lord wants it done, must be given voluntarily. There has been,*

and will be, no promiscuous solicitation of funds," Waltrip stated.

"About Tuesday of last week, I felt definitely led to fast and pray until not less than $5,000 came in to save my borrowing any more money to complete the first unit of Radio Chapel. I kept asking myself, 'If God would have to answer prayer to pay that money back later, why shouldn't He answer prayer for it now?' I got to where I couldn't eat without feeling convicted for it. Last Sunday, I made a covenant that I would pray and fast until He sent in all that I need at this time. So, in keeping that covenant, I have not eaten any food or taken any nourishment and will not until God keeps the covenant I feel He has made with me.

"This is the first time in my life that I have ever done such a thing. I never had any desire to do so. But I believe that the people of this community need to get over the spirit of dubiousness and doubt and realize that we can have a great independent evangelistic center here. I had a thousand times rather die than to see it fail in its completion."

"Fasting," it was stated by Mr. Williams, "is a fundamental doctrine and was practiced by the Lord Himself. Christ Himself fasted and prayed 40 days and 40 nights in the Wilderness."

Mr. Waltrip is continuing his daily broadcasts over KGLO each weekday morning at 9:15 and preaching each night except Monday in the Radio Chapel tent.

"I will keep going until I drop, or God sends in the five thousand," he stated. "But I don't believe for one moment

*that He will fail me. I am more than willing to stake my life
on that."*

It was during those seasons of Burroughs' fasts that Kathryn's
preaching schedule exploded. In addition to the church in Denver
and her crusades, she found herself conducting services daily at
Radio Chapel, sometimes as many as three per day, six days a week.
Kathryn loved to preach and she was never one to let a busy preaching schedule slow her down.

As the days grew colder and shorter and winter was approaching,
a steady crew of workmen diligently constructed the outer frame
and shell of the church. One day, before the frame was erected on
the finished foundation, Burroughs and Kathryn came to Keith with
an idea. After walking to the construction site, Burroughs opened
a small canvas bag and poured into their hands a number of brand
new 1937 half-dollar silver coins. Burroughs liked the fact that the
coins were emblazed with the words, "In God We Trust," and he
wanted to consecrate the Chapel foundation to God. Burroughs,
Kathryn, Keith, and Mary split the coins amongst themselves and
took turns walking to the four corners of the foundation, each of
them pausing to drop a coin into the corner bricks of Radio Chapel's
foundation. Keith recalled the construction workers observing their
activities and telling him their plan was "a great idea."

There developed an incredible closeness and camaraderie among
the four preachers, and it grew day by day. "It was the revival meetings of those days that drew us together," Mary recalled. "Burroughs
and Kathryn had a capability of reaching out to people, and people

would stand on their heads for them as a result. I really believe that. They were very loving and personable people to you." Every day was an exciting day. The building was taking shape. People were being saved. Vision was being cast. And of course, persecution was steadily increasing as it always does against the servants of God. Keith recalled that the larger the Chapel frame became, the larger the crowd of hecklers became as well. Historically, the vision God gives man is always met with some type of venom.

On Saturday, December 4, 1937, the local newspaper published the Articles of Incorporation for Radio Chapel. The official name of the corporation was listed as Radio Chapel Incorporate, with the place of address being given as, "located in the city of Mason City, Cerro Gordo County, Iowa." Thirty-seven people were invited to serve on the Board of Directors for the ensuing year. These individuals were from a variety of different backgrounds and denominational affiliations. Article III of the Incorporation defined the purpose and objects of Radio Chapel:

> "The purpose and objects of this corporation shall be of a religious, charitable, evangelistic character, having for the principal purpose the winning of souls and the establishment of the people's hearts in sound Christian truths. The program to be conducted shall be entirely undenominational and with absolutely no membership, where interested people of all denominations shall receive the finest type of Bible training and ministerial instruction regardless of their ability to pay; for the promotion of companionship, spiritual fellowship among the people of the community; to receive and disburse voluntary

contributions from the interested people; to establish, regulate, and control, and furnish rituals, forms, ceremonies, cards, supplies, and, certificates; to provide necessary symbols and signs of identification; to extend relief and aid to people; to have and hold religious and social gatherings and meetings; to improve the intellectual, moral and spiritual welfare of the interested people through Bible studies, lectures, ceremonies, and mutual visitation, and through any other means which will operate to improve the intellectual, moral, and spiritual welfare of the interested people."

Chapter Five

THE RADIO CHAPEL MAGAZINE

**Like cold water to a thirsty soul, so is good news from
a far country.**

Proverbs 25:25 (ESV)

Radio Chapel launched a bimonthly mailer called the *Radio Chapel Monthly Magazine* in December 1937. It was subtitled the "Official Organ of The House that God Built." The pamphlet-sized magazine, 16 pages in length, consisted of articles and sermons from a number of contributors, including Burroughs Waltrip, Kathryn Kuhlman, and Keith Williams. It was printed locally, supported by advertising from area businesses and services, and distributed to the growing attendees and supporters of Radio Chapel. In addition to sermons and articles, recipients of the mailer were also introduced to poetry, ministry notifications, current events, teachings, songs, and missionary updates.

Keith and Mary both agreed that one of the highlights of their time at the Chapel was the production of the magazine alongside Burroughs and Kathryn. Many of the articles were co-written with one another, and it was not unusual to find all four ministers collaborating with each other late into the night. A number of sermons and messages were subsequently birthed out of these spontaneous writing sessions.

The first edition of the magazine, Volume 1: Number 1, was printed shortly before Christmas, 1937. The front cover greeted readers with these words:

Merry Christmas and Happy New Year, Everybody!

To the great host of friends God has so wonderfully given us these past few months, and to the many, many more whom we would like so much to have as our friends, we want to say from the bottom of our heart and mean it with all the force of real friendship, "Merry Christmas and Happy New Year!"

May it be the earnest desire of each of us to attain more and more to the likeness of Him Whose birthday we lovingly commemorate. And may it become our consuming passion in 1938 to win more precious souls to Him than we ever have before.

Mary shared of Kathryn's great fondness for writing and her passion for choosing just the right words to "win more precious souls" to Christ. "I remember seeing Kathryn kneeling at the chair by her desk," she said. "She sought God for just the right words to say. She was very particular about finding the right words and the right way to say things. I recall her crying many times, not of sadness, but crying as she searched for just the best way to say things. That was very important to her."

Kathryn was in Mason City as much as her busy schedule would allow. She travelled constantly as she made her way from meeting to meeting, all the while continuing to oversee her growing church in Denver. "The idea of sending out a monthly magazine actually came up back during the tent meetings," Keith shared. "Both of them (Burroughs and Kathryn) were dead set on how important it was to put the Gospel in the mailboxes of people. Kathryn felt mailers worked really well in Denver, and it would be successful here as well." According to Mary, it was very important to their ministry team that God's people received regular and in-depth teaching rooted in solid Bible doctrine. The Radio Chapel magazine did not disappoint. According to Mary, Christmas was Kathryn's favorite time of the year. Therefore, the first collaborative article published in Radio Chapel's inaugural magazine was titled, "The Mystery of Christmas."

The Mystery of Christmas

How very many times have we read and marveled at that meaningful statement of Luke 2:7, "And she brought forth her firstborn son, and wrapped him in swaddling clothes, and laid him in a manger; because there was no room for them in the inn." Like a ray of light playing over a tray of precious jewels do the flashes of the Spirit's illumination point out the blessed truths here set forth.

Weary months. Months of wondering, dreaming, questioning, longing, and waiting. Months have passed. Mary folds to her bosom the most precious bundle ever cuddled to a mother's heart. He was her firstborn. Every instinct of motherhood came to the fore to make the moment one she would never forget. No wonder there was a soft glow in her eyes and a gentle cooing in her voice. But, remember too, that Mary knew that her firstborn was also the firstborn of God. He was not only her Son. He was God's Son.

Hid in her heart were the many things she had learned from the Angel of Annunciation, from her husband, Joseph, and from the hearing of the Sacred Script in the Synagogue. She knew her child was to die, because God must offer His Son as a sacrifice for the sins of the world. With what mingled feeling of joy and sorrow she must have dressed the tiny Bud of Blessedness that first day. He was not to be wrapped in the colorful garments she would have chosen. He was not born to live. He was born to die. So this beautiful young Jewess with eyes that must have welled with unshed tears took the bandages of burial and wrapped them about the soft, yielding body of her child, His Child. She knew He was to die, but she did not know that He would be a grown man, God's Man, when He died.

It is altogether likely that in the earlier days of her preparation for the coming of the Babe, Mary had prepared a little cradle that Joseph had carefully fashioned with the skill of his trade. She had lined and padded it with all the loving care she felt gently arising from an anointed heart. But the day of His birth has arrived. The little cradle is back in Nazareth. With utmost care she fashions the straw, clean straw that Joseph places within easy reach of her hands, and forms the first bed her son, His Son, was to know on earth. How little she was able to realize that He was to be the Humble One.

Was that welcome that Jesus received at His birth a foreshadowing of His treatment at the hands of the world? Has it not always been too busy to receive Him? Is it not too full of its own cares and pleasures to make room for Him? The little inn was much as the big world, crowded. But there were those who did receive Him, who did welcome Him: loving ones, and wise ones.

But the greatest mystery of all, let us mention it for a moment of meditation this Christmastime. The greatest mystery was the wrapping of Life in death. The Spirit of Everlasting Life was enfolded in death. What a Mystery! There is much about it that man can never understand this side of the Infinite Land, but he can know that the Life made possible the resurrection and glorification of that which had been death. So does the Seed of Life planted in our hearts by His Spirit bring forth a Life Everlasting.

Burroughs, Kathryn, and Keith all were careful to intertwine the great theme of God's love into the articles they wrote and the messages they spoke. For Kathryn especially, the love of God toward mankind was a frequent topic, and it wasn't uncommon to find her preaching with passion and conviction on the subject matter. Kathryn felt that the love of God, which was extended toward mankind as a result of Christ's sacrifice, should be declared from the rooftops. Whether it was in her campaigns, extensive revival crusades, or preaching at Radio Chapel, Kathryn patterned many of her sermons around the burden of sharing God's love. The article, "Because I Want To," was adapted from a sermon Kathryn had taught at a campaign in Detroit, Michigan.

Because I Want To

Our hearts have been strangely touched and our thinking inspired for days past now by the subject to which we are calling your attention tonight: Love Impelling. The subject might cover any one of several discussions. We might very fruitfully talk to you about God's love for the sinner. We might preach upon the golden text, John 3:16:

For God so loved the world, that he gave his only begotten Son, that whosoever believeth in him should not perish, but have everlasting life.

John 3:16 (KJV)

We might also use for our theme Ephesians 3:19 and talk about the love of God that is inconceivable:

And to know the love of Christ, which passeth knowledge, that ye might be filled with all the fulness of God.

Ephesians 3:19 (KJV)

We might use any one of several texts. We might turn over and use Jeremiah 31:3 and talk to you about the everlasting love of God for His saints, we might tell you tonight that it is an everlasting, eternal, unceasing love that God has for His people, this love that God has for them who are His:

The LORD hath appeared of old unto me, saying, Yea, I have loved thee with an everlasting love: therefore with lovingkindness have I drawn thee.

Jeremiah 31:3 (KJV)

We might go back to Deuteronomy 7:8 and talk to you about the sovereign love of God for His people, that He is a great and righteous King and this kingly love is the sovereign love that He gives so freely to His own:

But because the LORD loved you, and because he would keep the oath which he had sworn unto your fathers, hath the LORD brought you out with a mighty hand, and redeemed you out of the house of bondmen, from the hand of Pharaoh king of Egypt.

Deuteronomy 7:8 (KJV)

We might turn to Hosea 14:4 and talk about the free and undeserved love of God to those who are His:

I will heal their backsliding, I will love them freely: for mine anger is turned away from him.

Hosea 14:4 (KJV)

I'm sure that we will never get to the place, even after we are glorified, we will never get to the place where we feel that we are worthy of the love of God. Surely all during those ages with Jesus in Glory we will marvel at the way God loves us, and we will know that God's love is undeserved. Then I might go over to John 13:1 and talk to you about the unchanging love of God:

Now before the feast of the passover, when Jesus knew that his hour was come that he should depart out of this world unto the Father, having loved his own which were in the world, he loved them unto the end.

John 13:1 (KJV)

I think that in these last days we should appreciate that more than ever before. Natural love is backing down. There are very few homes today where the husband and the wife love each other like they should; father and son like they should; where the mother and daughter understand and truly love each other. But thank God there is a love that is unchanging; there is a love that is sure and secure. A love that no matter what the strain; no matter what the trial; no matter what the struggle; there is love that is immutable, that is unchanging, that you can depend upon. I might use Proverbs 8:31 for my text and talk to you about the serene love of God, that peaceful love of God:

Rejoicing in the habitable part of his earth; and my delights were with the sons of men.

Proverbs 8:31 (KJV)

Wherever you find God's love in abundance, you will always find tranquility. Wherever you find God's love present, you will also find peace. God never comes bringing division. God never brings division among His people. He comes when they are all of one accord; also visits us with an outpouring of divine peace, does this coming of the love of God.

I might also turn to 1 John 4:16 and talk to you about the boundless and the infinite love of God; a love that can't be drawn on too much; a love of which you can't require too much; a love that you can't limit to any portion of your life or to any particular time of need; a love that is so boundless that whatever the time and whatever the place and whatever the need, it is more than sufficient for that time, for that place, and for that need; an infinite love, not a love finite, but a love of that works beyond our asking; a love that gives beyond our understanding; a boundless and infinite love:

And we have known and believed the love that God hath to us. God is love; and he that dwelleth in love dwelleth in God, and God in him.

1 John 4:16 (KJV)

I am not going to use one of those texts, however, but, recognizing that God's loving us makes our love for Him possible, I am going to talk to you a little while about our love for God, using as my text John 14:23:

Jesus answered and said unto him, If a man love me, he will keep my words: and my Father will love him, and we will come unto him, and make our abode with him.

John 14:23 (KJV)

Now, I want to give you some points of clarification as I get into the message. The meaning of our subject is simply this: First, love, in the Scripture, is finding a great delight in something or someone. In other words, when you love God, you come to the place where you take a great delight in

God. Second, is the word "impelling." I want you to remember that this word comes from the Latin word "impello" and this in turn comes from the two Latin words, the first one in which we find, means "on" and the other "pelo" which means to "urge." In other words, the word impelling means "to drive" or "to urge on." Then together the words "love impelling" mean that kind of love that drives one on. It is that kind of love that urges you, that pushes you, that causes you to do things. That is love impelling. Now the proper setting for a love like that, a love that forces, drives, urges, is a heart filled with God's presence, and that in turn is a heart that delights in the love of God—our hearts are emptied and God fills them with divine love and that love does something to us that makes us love God and manifest that love in doing the things of God.

My text goes on to point out, in the first place, that our love for the Lord urges us to keep His Word. It tells us that if we really love the Lord, we are going to do what the Lord wants us to do; if we really love the Lord, we are going to say things that the Lord wants us to say; if we really love the Lord, we are going to be like the Lord said for us to be, and that is what it means. Now, the Psalmist had this thought a long time before when he declared:

Thy word have I hid in mine heart, that I might not sin against thee.

Psalm 119:11 (KJV)

I tell you, when you really get God's love in your heart, it urges you to be careful about going into sin. It is a mighty

74

constraining influence when you start to go into sin. It will help you to determine not to.

I want to give you several ways in which, by loving the Lord, we are urged to keep His Word. We are going to hold true to every single word of Jesus Christ as a Holy Word, that everything that the Lord said is to be taken as being entirely true without any trace of error; hold unquestionably they are authoritative and can be accepted and depended upon with all of our hearts. I hold that what Jesus said, God said, because I hold that Jesus is and ever will be God. We keep the word of the Lord in the sense that we adapt them to the clearest possible understanding and application.

Now you hear a great deal of the Gospel, but you do very little about it. You have heard and read and memorized great portions of the Scripture during your lifetime, but you have not done those words. We are told in the Word of God:

Therefore to him that knoweth to do good, and doeth it not, to him it is sin.

James 4:17 (KJV)

We are needing, in these days, to keep the word of the Lord in the sense of seeking and understanding it. What Jesus meant is, we are given that understanding and we are to apply those words, that understanding, to our daily lives and to the eternal hope that we have in God.

We then keep these words of the Lord by conducting every department of our lives according to them. You can't keep the words of the Lord and not serve Him every day of your life. There must be no part of your life void of the *touch of Jesus Christ if you are to keep His Word, because in His teachings is the revelation of God's will. The teachings of Jesus are such that every single part of your life has been definitely and clearly touched upon. There is no phase of it, no part of it, that the Lord did not reveal the will of God as how to conduct it. That is true concerning our attitude towards ourselves. We are to consider ourselves as being unrighteous. We are to consider ourselves as wholly and entirely without worth or merit. We are to consider ourselves as being the object of God's mercy and God's grace. We are to consider ourselves as needing of Him that which we cannot provide for ourselves, but can only obtain through His Son Jesus Christ. We are to look upon Him with a spirit of great reverence.*

Our attitude toward God is affected by His works. It seems to me rather meaningful that Jesus spoke most reverently of the Father. I think some people make a very tragic mistake when they assume or presume an attitude of familiarity with the Lord. The Lord does want you to feel that He is near to you. He does want to be your friend; He does want to be so close to you, even closer than hands and feet. But never let your heart get to the place where your attitude toward God is not one of reverence, where you can't walk tenderly and reverently before Almighty God. You want to walk in the fear of God. It is against the modern teaching of psychology that one should fear anything, but it is mighty good teaching to fear God, and if people were afraid, they would live closer to God. We should be afraid to go against the will of God; we should be afraid to doubt God; we should be afraid, lest in doing so we grieve the Holy

Spirit of God and become the objects of God's wrath instead of being the objects of God's mercy and God's blessings.

Jesus, I think too, gives us a definite understanding of the attitude that we are to have toward the lost. I think that when the record of the church of Jesus Christ is completed, we are going to find that the greatest tragedy that we have ever taken part in will be the neglect of the lost by the professing church. God's people are not concerned as they ought to be. They are not burdened as God wants them to be for the lost men and women in the world. You can't stay true to Jesus Christ, you can't be where Jesus wants you to be and not be burdened for lost men and women. About the surest way to know a man's heart is right with God is to know he loves the lost. Whatever faults he may have, whatever shortcomings he may have, as certain as you claim the promise of God, just as certain is God going to keep that promise. The latch on God's heart opens for you when you praise and love Jesus. That is God's promise. When you go to Him loving His Son, His heart just swings wide open and anything you go to Him in the Name of Jesus for He will grant to you.

The love that impels us to such a degree that it urges us and forces us—that impelling love brings God to us. Now, love is God's "home atmosphere." When you get to Heaven, you are going to find there is an atmosphere of love up there. No malice, no jealousy will be there, but rather an atmosphere of love which is God, which is His natural sphere of habitation. So when you get that kind of love in your heart that urges you and compels you to do for the Lord because of your love for Him and not things, it urges you to turn your back on sin. Just as soon as you do that, it enables God to forgive you. I want to remind you that no matter how powerful the blood of Jesus Christ is, it is absolutely impossible for God to forgive an unconfessed sin. He can't forgive it unless it is confessed by you, but He does forgive it when confessed.

It works like this, your loving the Lord and believing Him enables Him to prove Himself. God is waiting to show you that every promise in the Book is true, but before God can prove that promise to you, you have got to believe Him enough to claim the promise. But just as because you have to, you must also establish in your heart a home atmosphere in which the Lord can dwell because that is the kind of love He is used to. He is accustomed to that kind of atmosphere. He loves us not because He has to, but because He wants to. Now that kind of love is the kind of love that God wants you to give Him. You just get that kind of home atmosphere and He will come and dwell in it.

Love is the expression of God's presence, and when you get to that place where love fills your heart, you know that the Lord is present there. You can't have the love of God without having God, and you can't have God without having the love of God, because this impelling love is the expression of God's presence.

Love is God's association. I think that one beautiful name for Him who sits at God's right hand tonight would be Love. I think certainly that one word description of Him who has on His brow the scar of the thorns and in His hands and feet the print of the nails and in His side the stamp of the spear head, would be the one word, Love. God is accustomed, I say, to the association of love. There is complete harmony, unity, accord, as love gives these things to the Father and the Son and the Holy Spirit. And that impelling love that urges you to lay your all on the altar because you love the Lord, gives you that association of a God who loves like that and gives God the association of a man or a woman who loves that way.

Love is God's reception. We can't see God in a heart that is filled with hate. You can't see Him in a heart that has malice toward another. The heart in which you receive God is a heart of love. God comes in that moment that you really give in to His love. Love is God's reception.

In closing, I want to tell you that this impelling love—this love that causes you to do, not because you have to, but because you want to, this love that forces you to do things just because you love so much you can't help yourself—that kind of love is a wonderful thing. Don't you think so? Beloved, the love that impels you to love the Lord with all of your heart, expels sin. Sin cannot stay in a heart like that. Just like light drives out darkness, so does love expel sin. It has to go.

Love that impels, repels. For when you love the Lord like that and with that kind of love, you are able to repel doubt, unbelief, worry. It is mighty hard for these things to get into a heart that is filled with love.

The love that impels, also compels. When you get a heart filled with love like that the flesh is compelled to be subject to the spirit. A lot of people wonder why it is that they don't have victory over the flesh and the things of the *flesh. The reason is that they just don't love God with that impelling love. When your heart is full of the love of the Lord, the old flesh has to surrender to the Spirit of God.*

The love that impels, propels. That is the kind of love that causes people to do things. That is why people pray when they do not have to. That is why people read the Bible when they don't have to. That is why people testify when they don't have to. That is why people go to God when things are discouraging them. The love that compels, propels.

The love that impels, impels. When your heart is filled with the love that causes you to lay your all on the altar for Jesus Christ, a love that forces you just because of love to make an absolute surrender of everything to God, this same love impels God. Not because He has to, not because we could make Him or would make Him, but because His love impels Him to open the windows of Heaven and pour out such a blessing that you are not able to contain it. God does all of this for us because of His impelling love toward us.

If you really love the Lord, you will keep His words and His Father will love you, and they will make their abode with you until you go to make your abode with them.

Chapter Six

AMERICA'S OUTSTANDING YOUNG WOMAN EVANGELIST

Even on my male servants and female servants in those days I will pour out my Spirit, and they shall prophesy.

Acts 2:18 (ESV)

In February 1938, Kathryn was once again in Denver. This time, however, she was taking a rest from her church and traveling responsibilities. Her most recent revival campaigns had taken her to Milwaukee, Detroit, Chicago, Minneapolis, and Peoria. Media outlets continued to describe her campaigns as "highly successful." A Detroit newspaper stated, "Miss Kuhlman is a very attractive young woman, charming and entertaining and possessing a remarkable personality, but whereas these qualities are of inestimable value, yet exceeding these are her ability as a speaker and her very deep sincerity and zeal for the work of God." Kathryn had become a media darling.

It was during this time of rest that Keith Williams summoned Kathryn back to Mason City to once again assist Burroughs in an additional fundraising effort during his second fast which he began earlier in the month. A new goal of $10,000 was designated to furnish the new opera seats as well as complete construction on the front of the church building, of which, up to the present time, $8,000 had been raised. Keith, who was now Radio Chapel's Assistant Director, stated, "We feel that we are fortunate in obtaining Miss Kuhlman, especially at this time. It so happened that she was on a rest period in her great Denver work and could accept my urgent call to come to Mason City on short notice. She is booked many months ahead in her work. We do not know how long Miss Kuhlman can stay in Mason City, but she is worthy of a packed house for every service and no doubt will have a great attendance every night." Returning to Iowa may have been inopportune, but Kathryn enjoyed great favor with the people of Mason City, and she very much enjoyed her developing relationship with Burroughs and Radio Chapel.

The *Globe Gazette*, which was very favorable to Kathryn at this time, was quick to remind its readers that Miss Kuhlman still continued to direct her own evangelist center in Colorado, the Denver Revival Tabernacle, which was one of the largest in the country. Interested readers were informed that she would be speaking in Mason City each night at 7:30 p.m., except for Monday night, when no service would be held. It was further announced that Kathryn would once again take charge of the musical program featuring Ralph Geer and assorted guest musicians.

Although Kathryn had been a vital part of Radio Chapel's pioneering and ministry since its inception, the *Globe Gazette* newspaper took special interest in her arrival for this series of meetings. Perhaps it was due to the vast amounts of money needed to be raised for the project. Quite possibly it was due to the "doubting Thomases" and critics who were now beginning to openly voice their suspicion and concerns over the purpose of Radio Chapel. Clearly there were those who began to suspect a romantic interest between Burroughs and Kathryn. The article that ran in the Saturday, February 19, 1938, edition of the *Globe Gazette* served as a window into Kathryn's heart regarding both her church in Denver and her work in Mason City:

> *An attractive young woman, nearly six feet tall, with blond, permanent waved hair and laughing eyes has come to Mason City to help Evangelist Burroughs A. Waltrip in his campaign at Radio Chapel.*
>
> *There is no permanent or romantic connection, however, it must be added. Miss Kathryn Kuhlman of Denver, Colorado, is scheduled to appear each evening and preach at the Radio Chapel during the next week only.*
>
> *She admitted that her coming at this particular time had some connection with Mr. Waltrip's fast, which now is in its third week since he announced that he had begun it in an effort to raise $10,000 for the completion of Radio Chapel.*

"I don't like to leave as long as he needs my help in the work here," she replied in answer to a question by the Globe Gazette reporter, "although my schedule calls for my presence in Denver at the end of next week."

She told of her own revival tabernacle in Denver which seats 2,000 persons and is nearly always full for her meetings. Her work there has been developed in the last four years, she said, and she personally attends to all of the details in connection with its administration including business, program arrangement and sermons.

When the reporter expressed surprise that such an attractive young woman should still be single at the age of 25, she smiled and then pondered for a moment before answering.

"Perhaps it is because my time is so entirely occupied with my work. Does that make you smile? It really must be true, however, for I don't pretend to be different from others. But I would make many sacrifices for my work. You know, I am constantly striving against the attitude in the people I meet that I am just another preacher. I am just as human as anyone and I certainly don't want to be regarded in that way."

She went on to say that because of her constant contacts with high school and college students who come to her with their problems during her meetings with them, she is often regarded as "ultra modern," but she also informed the reporter that she is the only woman member of the Fundamentalist Ministers Union as well as a member of the International Ministerial Union.

She explained that she started her evangelistic work at the age of 14 and has been at it constantly ever since, averaging more than 500 sermons every year.

"Perhaps a man would find it almost too strenuous, being married to one with my schedule," she laughed.

Within two days, the additional funds were raised and the goal of $10,000 was met, yet the skeptics raged on. Burroughs stated that during his period of fasting, criticism poured in on him "like a flood." He continued, "Even many of my best friends could not understand. I knew God was with me, and I thank Him there was never a minute's doubt."

During one of the many times Keith and I discussed and reflected back upon Radio Chapel, he shared how people who were walking by began to jeer and hurl criticisms at the workers and staff during the early days of construction. "You could tell there was a lot of jealousy out there. People didn't like how fast the work was growing and they didn't like that people were leaving their churches to go there. We had spies coming to our meetings and we knew it."

Burroughs found himself regularly defending both the fund-raising and outreach efforts of Radio Chapel. In the Wednesday, February 23, 1938, edition of the newspaper, he was quoted as saying, "Watch Radio Chapel and see what we do with the money in the next few months. Every penny of money we received is accounted for and an up-to-the-minute set of books is subject to regular audits. We give God all the glory, as the givers themselves want us to. I refused to give the city council a single name when I was trying to get my building permit. I challenged them as I now challenge all those who in the least question the fact that God honored faith and answered prayer for $10,000." Fractures in his favor with the city were frequently becoming evident, and battle lines were being drawn for what would prove to become future conflicts. Yet, none of these things affected the passions or pursuits of the Radio Chapel preaching team as they forged ahead with their vision for ministry. Through challenges and setbacks, Keith and Mary took close note of Kathryn's victorious attitude toward whatever came their way.

It was obvious that Keith had a remarkable respect for Kathryn Kuhlman. Both Keith and Mary did, but it was Keith who was assistant pastor to Kathryn. Sitting together in their modest home in Watertown, South Dakota, he communicated his fond affection for Kathryn's ministry style. "She was a very good preacher and sensitive in prayer," he said. "She was made for preaching, and her gift took over on the platform."

THE ORDINATION

Perhaps it was due in part to this ministerial bond that Kathryn was asked to conduct Keith's ordination service. Keith had served in the capacity of assistant pastor since October 1937. His ordination was held on Friday, February 25, 1938, in the recently completed Radio Chapel auditorium. The newspaper shared that Keith M. Williams, assistant director of Radio Chapel, was to be ordained to the Gospel ministry at a special service where Burroughs and Kathryn would serve as ordainers and speakers. Burroughs stated, "We are ordaining Mr. Williams to the sacred work of the Gospel ministry because of his and our firm conviction of God's call to him and his sincere desire to serve God and his fellowman in that capacity. He will continue as assistant director and special field representative of Radio Chapel with full ministerial authority." Ralph Geer, the Chapel's music director, once again provided the music, and Radio Chapel was beautifully decorated for the service. Kathryn was listed as an ordained minister who carried her credentials with the Fundamental Ministerial Association of America, and therefore bore full authority to conduct the ritual of ordination.

On Friday evening, a crowd of 700 people gathered for Keith's ordination in the sanctuary of Radio Chapel. In charge of the ordination were Miss Kathryn Kuhlman and Burroughs A. Waltrip. Burroughs presented a Bible to Keith as a token of ordination and Kathryn presented a large basket of white American Beauty roses to Mary. Keith shared with those present about his decision to enter the ministry and his previous Gospel work before receiving ministry instructions from Burroughs. Kathryn then took charge of the service and, after laying hands on Keith and Mary, preached a sermon on the call to ministry.

Kathryn's charge to Keith was so well received that it was reprinted in the Radio Chapel bi-monthly magazine, which was mailed out at the end of February 1938. It reads:

> **I charge thee therefore before God, and the Lord Jesus Christ, who shall judge the quick and the dead at his appearing and his kingdom; Preach the word; be instant in season, out of season; reprove, rebuke, exhort with**

all longsuffering and doctrine. For the time will come when they will not endure sound doctrine; but after their own lusts shall they heap to themselves teachers, having itching ears; And they shall turn away their ears from the truth, and shall be turned unto fables. But watch thou in all things, endure afflictions, do the work of an evangelist, make full proof of thy ministry.

2 Timothy 4:1-5 (KJV)

This is a sacred hour. This call to the Gospel ministry is the most glorious thing in all of the world to me. It helps me to realize that God is just the same today. He is still seeking out those who will be faithful to Him in this great business of soul-winning. This call reminds us that there is a real and personal relationship with God. It also brings us face to face with the fact of our personal responsibility to God.

The hour's great need is for a true Church of Jesus Christ. Let us get away from the organizations of men with their peculiar creeds and religious formulas. Let us realize that the true Church, the real Church of Jesus Christ, is the body of the "blood washed," and that Jesus Christ is Head over all things and the Church; that we owe full allegiance to the true Church, and wholehearted participation in her commission.

Take heed therefore unto yourselves, and to all the flock, over the which the Holy Ghost hath made you overseers, to feed the church of God, which he hath purchased with his own blood.

Acts 20:28 (KJV)

We believe with all our heart in a God-called ministry. May God save us in these last days from a ministry of professionalism. May we be delivered from the ecclesiastical hirelings that men can buy to preach according to their own creeds and systems of belief. And may God grant our pulpits freedom from man-controlled sermonizers, freedom from handbooks and manuals of prepared sermons. God is not calling men and women to ministries of expedience, but of obedience and truth.

The New Testament ministry is one of absolute independence, so far as man is concerned, but one of complete dependence so far as God is concerned. We must wait upon God for humility; we must lean upon Him for understanding; by His grace we must hold the flesh in subjection; and we must believe Him for our sustenance.

Our charge from God is to seek a Christ-honoring ministry. Certainly the true minister of the Gospel must live a Christ-centered life; his message must be Christ-exulting or it can never be soul-winning and soul-feeding; he must work only in His strength; and the difference in his life must not be one of clothes and frocks, but one of spirit.

Study to shew thyself approved unto God, a workman that needeth not to be ashamed, rightly dividing the word of truth.

2 Timothy 2:15 (KJV)

I charge thee: Win souls. Edify the believer.

Reverend Keith Williams was then ordained by Kathryn Kuhlman. She laid her hands upon him and delivered to him the charge for his life's ministry. She anointed him and shared her mantle with him. When I asked Keith what that meant to him, he paused for a long time and then said, "It was one of the greatest days of my life."

The cover page of the February 1938 Radio Chapel monthly magazine announced the ordination service to the residents of the Heartland. "Keith M. Williams, Radio Chapel's assistant director, has been ordained to the Gospel ministry. In a beautiful service of ordination in Radio Chapel on the evening of February 25, Burroughs A. Waltrip and Kathryn Kuhlman, by the laying on of hands, consecrated Keith M. Williams, assistant director, to the Gospel ministry. A great congregation filled the auditorium beyond seating capacity for the service."

Pointing at a picture from the ordination service, Mary commented, "Look at the crowd we had sitting on benches. We didn't have all the chairs at the time, so we had to squeeze everybody in like we did. We were fortunate to have lived when and where it all happened," she said cheerfully. Keith continued, "People believed in Radio Chapel wholeheartedly, but it's because they believed in the leaders of Radio Chapel. They were great leaders and had a great way about them."

Chapter Seven

How Old Are You?

When I was a child, I talked like a child, I thought like a child, I reasoned like a child. When I became a man, I put the ways of childhood behind me.

1 Corinthians 13:11 (NIV)

"I think she was such a lovely lady. We were so very much friends with her," explained Mary as we talked together. "Kathryn had a lot of the Holy Spirit when she was on the platform. And she dressed so beautifully. She wore a special gown, a special garment because she felt it was more spiritual." Not surprisingly, the striking style and substance of Kathryn's ministry so impacted Keith and Mary that seventy years later they still spoke of her as if they were in one of Kathryn's crusades just last week.

Kathryn preached on every topic imaginable, and she preached with passion. Her subject matters included Christian living, forgiveness, the end times, life's decisions, and the tactics of Satan. And of course, she loved to preach about the Holy Spirit. Mary continued, "We had good meetings at Radio Chapel. Exceptional meetings. The power of prayer was just wonderful there." Prayer, praise, and preaching are three essential components to a move of God, and a move of God was what Radio Chapel was experiencing. It wasn't uncommon for the evening service to go well past midnight as people everywhere would come to partake of the spiritual food being offered by the gifted Radio Chapel preaching team.

On Saturday, March 19, 1938, the newspaper reported that Kathryn would once again head up the local campaign. Kathryn had been in Denver attending to the cares of her church following Keith's ordination, yet now, without even one month having passed, she was on her way back to Mason City. It was becoming clear that churchgoers in the Heartland could not get enough of Kathryn Kuhlman's ministry. Helen Gulliford, her evangelistic pianist, traveled with Kathryn to assist in the meetings, which also included the musical services of Ralph Geer and Harry D. Clark, Billy Sunday's former song leader.

"Knowing the evangelistic work as I do, I feel that it would be absolutely impossible to obtain the services of a more effective evangelistic team than Miss Kuhlman, Mr. Clarke, and Miss Gulliford," Burroughs stated. "We have the greatest opportunity for a truly great revival campaign that North Iowa has had in many years." The *Globe Gazette* reported, "Miss Kuhlman attracted capacity attendance during a short campaign which she conducted toward the close of the recent season of prayer and fasting in which Mr.

Waltrip was engaged a month ago. Her return campaign is in answer to an insistent public demand."

It was in this environment of expectancy that Kathryn's gifts would brilliantly shine. Her messages were passionate and challenging, well thought out, and delivered with enthusiasm. It was with an ardent zeal that Kathryn took the platform that Sunday afternoon and preached this sermon before a capacity crowd. Her message was titled "How Old Are You?"

How Old Are You?

Does it pay to be an out-and-out Christian, as far as Heaven is concerned? Will the lukewarm, carnal, worldly Christians be just as well off in Heaven as the spiritual, prayerful, soul-winning Christians? Will Abraham be any better off in Heaven than Lot? Will it make any difference in Heaven that Paul, "finished the course and kept the faith," and that Demas, "hath forsaken me, having loved this present world"? Does it pay to be a Christian? Does it pay to be an out-and-out Christian? Does it pay today? Will it pay tomorrow? In Heaven?

What do such passages as the following mean if Heaven does not reveal a difference between Christians?

But lay up for yourselves treasures in heaven, where neither moth nor rust doth corrupt, and where thieves do not break through nor steal.

Matthew 6:20 (KJV)

Blessed are ye, when men shall hate you, and when they shall separate you from their company, and shall reproach you, and cast out your name as evil, for the Son of man's sake. Rejoice ye in that day, and leap for joy: for, behold, your reward is great in heaven: for in the like manner did their fathers unto the prophets.

Luke 6:22-23 (KJV)

How does this happen? By living a good and separated Christian life and service unto the Lord. If we reject the fact that it pays in Heaven to have been a separated Christian here, we must explain away these and many other similar clear and definite promises in God's Word.

Now, we ask you to carefully notice the following scriptures, for in them we will find the truth that we will be of varying ages in Heaven and will have vastly different degrees of joy there. These passages will also reveal how old we will be in Heaven. Listen to this first portion of the Word:

Wherefore laying aside all malice, and all guile, and hypocrisies, and envies, and all evil speakings, As newborn babes, desire the sincere milk of the word, that ye may grow thereby.

1 Peter 2:1-2 (KJV)

Now, notice that those whom Peter addressed were old in the flesh, old enough for malice, guilt, hypocrisies, and envies, but still they were babes in the spirit. Now we know there is a physical life and a spiritual life. Christians have both at the same time, even though their ages in each are different. In other words, we may be old physically, but a babe spiritually. How many of God's children have been saved for many years but they are still babes in Christ?

Of whom we have many things to say, and hard to be uttered, seeing ye are dull of hearing. For when for the time ye ought to be teachers, ye have need that one teach you again which be the first principles of the oracles of God; and are become such as have need of milk, and not of strong meat. For every one that useth milk is unskilful in the word of righteousness: for he is a babe. But strong meat belongeth to them that are of full age, even those who by reason of use have their senses exercised to discern both good and evil.

Hebrews 5:11–14 (KJV)

In this scripture, the writer calls a second truth to our attention, namely, that a Christian may have been saved for many years, but with no growth. They have remained a babe in Christ, even though they are old physically. They have been saved long enough to be a teacher, but they are still a babe in Christ.

Time does not indicate how old you are spiritually. Even though you testify of being saved forty years, if you haven't grown spiritually, then you are but a babe in Christ. This same truth is emphasized as clearly in still another passage.

And I, brethren, could not speak unto you as unto spiritual, but as unto carnal, even as unto babes in

Christ. I have fed you with milk, and not with meat: for hitherto ye were not able to bear it, neither yet now are ye able. For ye are yet carnal: for whereas there is among you envying, and strife, and divisions, are ye not carnal, and walk as men?

1 Corinthians 3:1–3 (KJV)

And now listen again to what keeps them from becoming mature, well-fed Christians. "For ye are yet carnal: for whereas there is among you envying, and strife, and divisions, are ye not carnal, and walk as men?" Here we have Christians who have been saved long enough to be eating spiritual meat, but instead just have the milk. Milk is for babes.

Now, we have seen three facts established: First, there is a physical life and a spiritual life. Second, Christians have both the physical and the spiritual life at the same time. Third, the physical age is different from the spiritual age.

The spiritual, Heavenly, or eternal life begins with a birth the same as the physical and earthly life begins with a birth. The spiritual and eternal life is not reformation, nor confirmation, nor being baptized, nor joining the church. We get our spiritual life the moment we are born again.

Jesus answered and said unto him, Verily, verily, I say unto thee, Except a man be born again, he cannot see the kingdom of God.

John 3:3 (KJV)

The moment we are born again, we are "babes in Christ." Consequently, we need to grow in grace and in the knowledge of our Lord and Savior Jesus Christ.

Again, a baby in the physical life grows according to physical laws. So also in the spiritual life, newborn babes grow according to spiritual laws. A child five years old should be a certain height and weight. A young man of sixteen years of age should be a certain height and weight. They have both grown according to their age. However, age or time does not determine spiritual growth. All have seen some who, two weeks after conversion and being born again, have become soul winners, separated unto God and well-versed in the Bible. On the other hand, some who have been saved forty years have not grown a bit.

How old are you spiritually? Or, in that eternal life which you already have, are you a babe in Christ? Have you grown so that you are a spiritual boy? Or are you full-grown into the stature of Christ?

Till we all come in the unity of the faith, and of the knowledge of the Son of God, unto a perfect man, unto the measure of the stature of the fullness of Christ: That we henceforth be no more children, tossed to and fro, and carried about with every wind of doctrine, by the sleight of men, and cunning craftiness, whereby they lie in wait to deceive; But speaking the truth in love, may grow up into him in all things, which is the head, even Christ.

Ephesians 4:13-15 (KJV)

Perhaps you have already discovered your spiritual age. Well, I believe the following will bring to us a true realization of how old we are spiritually.

There are two things that every parent waits so anxiously for their child to do—walk and talk. I have watched with amusement my loved ones and friends seeking to teach their little ones how to take their first step. They hold their arms and swing their legs in an attempt to teach them to walk.

The Bible speaks time and time again of the Christian walk. Spiritual babes cannot walk. Thus, if you are not able to walk the Christian walk, perhaps you are yet a babe in Christ. How are you getting along in your Christian walk?

Wherein in time past ye walked according to the course of this world.

Ephesians 2:2 (KJV)

Have you ever watched a mother or daddy helping their little one to talk? How often times, we try to have them say "mama" or "dada"? Sometimes, the child will say "mama" first, and sometimes he will say "dada" first. How we cherish those first baby words.

We write down in the baby book when he took the first step and when he spoke the first word. So, the Heavenly Father awaits the first words of prayer from His child. Have you learned how to talk yet? How to talk to your Heavenly Father in prayer? If not, perhaps you have not grown and are still a babe in Christ.

Babes always need special attention. They fuss at the slightest annoyances. A sure sign of spiritual babyhood is the "crybaby" instinct towards everything which seems to go wrong in the church. They are easily offended and always feel someone has slighted them. They wrestle with jealousy. They always feel the pastor has hurt them. Spoiled babies must always have their way. Dear Christian, it is a serious thing to remain a baby in Christ. How old do you think you are by now?

If you haven't discovered your spiritual age as of yet, let me ask you a few questions. Are you able to study and feed on God's Word yet? Babies always need to be fed. They need to be spoon-fed. Their milk needs to be warmed. How every pastor tries to nourish new children, giving them just the right food to get them to grow so they will study the Word of God for themselves.

Are you still in spiritual babyhood? Must the sermons be just the right kind or you are not interested? Or is it that once a year the evangelist comes around and gives you some warm milk with a bit of honey and gets you fattened up and your cheeks bloom out, but a month later you are right back on your starvation diet? Beloved, it is a serious thing not to grow spiritually and to remain a spiritual babe, immature and undernourished.

Reflecting back, Keith recollected how Kathryn would stay after service and fellowship with the people until they all had left. She could be found talking and laughing with people one moment and praying fervently with them the next. This is what made her so unique. This is why people loved her. She was celebrated not just for her calling, but also for her genuineness. "And then the four of us would go out for coffee and fellowship," Mary shared. "We would do that every weekday. We had wonderful times together. We had good times together! It was a privilege."

Chapter Eight

PASSION FOR PREACHING

His word is in my heart like a fire, a fire shut up in my bones.

Jeremiah 20:9 (NIV)

My time with Keith and Mary Williams was much more than the proverbial trip down memory lane. Our discussions lasted for hours as we talked about the glory and energy of those revival days. Actually, they talked and I listened. The privilege afforded to me was a rare one, and I knew it. It seemed as though these two aged saints had waited a lifetime to be able to tell their stories, and now was their chance. The floodgates of their memories opened as they shared story after story of their time at Radio Chapel with Burroughs Waltrip and Kathryn Kuhlman. And we didn't just talk about Radio Chapel. We talked about revival. We talked about how wildly popular revivals were in days gone by, and they reminisced to me regarding the ache in their hearts to see those days again.

Kathryn was a revivalist in every sense of the word. She believed in revival. She preached revival. She hungered for revival. And she preached in a way that stirred up the hearts of her listeners for revival. Between her ministerial duties at Denver Revival Tabernacle and Radio Chapel, Kathryn kept herself busy conducting crusades in many of the surrounding towns and cities.

On May 18, 1938, the *Waterloo Daily Courier* ran a story announcing a series of nightly meetings to be held at Clark's Tabernacle in Waterloo, Iowa, a campaign that was scheduled to run until June 1. The article referred to Kathryn as "the youthful evangelist from Denver, Colorado," where "her congregation had swelled to almost 3,000 church attendees." Harry Clark was the song leader for Kathryn's campaigns in Mason City, and he also ministered with her at a revival campaign she conducted in November 1937 at the Metropolitan Tabernacle in Detroit, Michigan.

As usual, Kathryn's meetings were met with great success. The main auditorium was filled every night with latecomers forced to stand in the rear. On May 22, 1938, the *Waterloo Daily Courier* published a follow-up article in the midst of her revival meetings.

Many great speakers of America and abroad have been brought to the city of Waterloo by Reverend Harry D. Clarke, founder and pastor of Clarke Tabernacle. Rev. Clarke feels that the tabernacle occupies the same place as the lighthouse does in the ocean, therefore, the lights shine out every night in the week and many souls tossed about by the storms of life have found refuge and peace in this wooden haven of rest. It is safely estimated that there has been a conversion for every day of the year. At present for two weeks Kathryn Kuhlman of Denver, Colorado, is the guest speaker. She has a strong personality and is an untiring worker for God. Everyone is welcome to attend the splendid preaching mission.

It was with this strong personality that Kathryn would simultaneously challenge and persuade the hearts of men and women everywhere. Keith said it was like that at every one of her meetings. "We went to Kathryn's revival meetings before she came to help start our church. We attended at least three or four of them. She was an excellent preacher."

"The Evidences of Conversion" was a comprehensive sermon of Kathryn's that Keith had a special affinity for. In this message, Kathryn powerfully and eloquently describes the fruit that clearly distinguishes the saved from the lost. The sermon so impacted Keith that, after receiving it from Kathryn in 1939, he preached it 49 times over the next 25 years.

The Evidences of Conversion

There are two messages which are of vital importance and need to be proclaimed today as never before in the history of this old world. The first of these messages which must be preached as never before is the message of salvation by grace, in order that those teeming thousands who are still under the bondage of sin may know the one way of life and be saved before it is everlastingly too late.

The other message which needs to be preached, and the one the Good Lord has laid upon my heart for you who are gathered here this evening, is dealing in a very practical way with the evidences of conversion, so that each of you may know here and now whether you are saved, or whether you stand in need of grace.

Examine yourselves, whether ye be in the faith; prove your own selves. Know ye not your own selves, how that Jesus Christ is in you, except ye be reprobates?

2 Corinthians 13:5 (KJV)

This most challenging text pleadingly exhorts you to examine yourselves to see if you are in the faith. We are living in a day when the line of demarcation between the saved and the lost is scarcely visible because of the worldliness that has permeated the church. This is most challenging.

We will consider this text from three points of view: First, the assurance of salvation. Second, the fruits of faith. Third, the marks which distinguish the saved from the lost. These are solemn truths, and I sincerely trust we will examine our hearts and judge ourselves now, thus escaping the judgment to come.

The assurance of salvation is the evidence to yourself that you are a Christian. The fruits of faith plainly present the proof of our salvation to others. The marks which distinguish the saved from the lost will reestablish the almost completely obliterated line of demarcation between the saved and the lost so that all of you may know, here and now, where you stand with God and in the light of His Word.

I am well aware that a great majority of people today think it rather presumptuous for any of us to say that we know we are saved. Most of them are laboring under the delusion that no man can, nor will know until the day of judgment, whether or not they are saved. But, throughout the Scriptures, there is no such foundation for believing such a conclusion. In fact, I know that I am saved. Sad to say, this teaching has not only filtered into the minds of men, but also into the pulpits of our land. May God help us to expose this lie that has been emitted from the pit.

Let us study the Word and study a few of the passages from which we receive our assurance. Romans 8:16 declares, "The Spirit itself beareth witness with our spirit, that we are the children of God." The promise is not that "we may" or "we shall be," but God says emphatically, "we are the children of God."

Perhaps the experience of another will help us. A pastor went into a home calling upon an aged lady, just ready to pass on. Her heart was gripped with fear as she thought of death and, even though she had accepted the Lord Jesus Christ while a girl, to think she might at last be lost and spend eternity in Hell was more than she could bear. The pastor was tenderly sympathetic and sought earnestly to persuade her and comfort her. Desperately they prayed, but seemingly to no avail. Then, just ready to leave, the pastor casually mentioned how happy he was that he could come into her home and what a lovely home she had. She proudly remarked that it was all her own.

The pastor caught the strain of her thought and inquired, "How do you know it is yours?" She replied, "Before my husband passed away three years ago, he made the last payment." The pastor replied, "Is that all you have to prove it is yours?" She answered, "Why, Pastor, I know it's mine because I have everything recorded in the courthouse." The pastor sat back down and said, "Well, that's fine, but if I can show you the record of your salvation in the Bible, would you believe that you were saved and ready?" The lady sat up a bit. "Why, of course I would. Is there such a record?" The pastor smiled. "Indeed there is. I'll just turn in your Bible for you to 1 John 5:10–12 to see what it tells us in plain language."

He that believeth on the Son of God hath the witness in himself: he that believeth not God hath made him a liar; because he believeth not the record that God gave of his Son. And this is the record, that God hath given to us eternal life, and this life is in his Son. He that hath the Son hath life; and he that hath not the Son of God hath not life.

1 John 5:10–12 (KJV)

A sigh of relief came forth from that frail body, and she was heard to say, "Thank you, Jesus. I believe."

I ask earnestly, do you have the Son of God as your personal Savior? Can you say with all sincerity of life, "I know whom I have believed?" Or, is there a doubt, a question? Are you anxious about your eternal welfare? Beloved, we can know. And you can know before you leave this church tonight that you are God's and He is yours.

Beloved, now are we the sons of God,

1 John 3:2 (KJV)

Sad to say, there are those who are literally entertaining false hopes of Heaven, being professors of religion only, with no possession of Christ for salvation. Many who are leaning on some form of worship, some ritual, some ceremony, some charitable deed instead of the Son of God.

How many today have been worked over by religion but have never been operated on by the Holy Ghost? Beloved, there is a difference, and it spells the difference between eternal life and eternal death, between Heaven or Hell. Our Lord spoke most seriously when He said:

Many will say to me in that day, Lord, Lord, have we not prophesied in thy name? and in thy name have cast out devils? and in thy name done many wonderful works?

Matthew 7:22 (KJV)

But, according to the Word, Jesus will say:

And then will I profess unto them, I never knew you: depart from me, ye that work iniquity.

Matthew 7:23 (KJV)

I ask you tonight with all the love of my heart, are you going to be one who will hear such an awful judgment, simply because you would not listen? I trust you will examine yourselves. Examine yourselves, whether you be in the faith. If any are entertaining false hopes of Heaven, I trust you will face this most important problem today.

And now, we turn to the proof of your salvation, or the fruits of faith. This is that which gives evidence of our salvation to others. We must ask some very pertinent questions. And, if you have at some time in your life made some definite move toward becoming a Christian, these are surely in the interest of your own soul. Let us search the depths of our sin-stained hearts and find the answers to these questions.

There are three proofs of your salvation. First, was your faith real faith? When you made that move toward becoming a Christian, perhaps as a child of tender years or when you faced a crisis, was the faith in which you took your stand a real stand in repentance and faith, or was it merely shallow believism? Was the act of decision a time of genuine repentance and then definite faith in the Lord Jesus Christ to forgive all your sins, or was it merely giving mental assent to knowledge that you have learned?

We are plagued in our America and in our generation with a message that sets aside the need of a genuine experience of repentance in favor of a message in shallow believism. Everybody believes, but everybody has not repented. With the hope of helping you to see the truth, allow me to pass on an experience from the life of a friend. A preacher was holding meetings in the south and during the course of the meeting, there were girls who sat in the back seats giggling and cutting up between themselves. The message made little impression and the altar call still less. Following the dismissal, they made their way out the door and down the steps to the street. However, the last girl was stopped by a lady of the church who asked her, "Are you a Christian?"

"Why, I don't know."

"Do you believe the Bible?"

"Oh, yes, I believe the Bible."

"Do you believe that Jesus died for all sinners and all who believe can be saved?"

"Yes, I believe that Jesus died on the cross."

"Well, if you believe the Bible and you believe that Jesus died on the cross for sinners, you must be a Christian, don't you think?"

"Why, yes, I guess I must be. Why, yes, I must be." Then running down the stairs to go with her friends, she threw up her arms and said, "Whee, I'm a Christian now. The lady told me so."

I have related this story in order that you may see that she was most assuredly not manifesting a saving knowledge of Christ, either in this experience or a previous one. There was no sorrow over the sin, nor was there repentance because of the sin. "Examine yourselves, whether ye be in the faith," the Bible reminds.

And now, secondly, did you accept Christ as your Savior? Probing just a little deeper, when you went through your motions of becoming a Christian, did you accept Christ as your Savior? Or did you merely join a church, which, I am sad to say, has been the damning experience of many thousands of church members?

"Believe on the Lord Jesus Christ and thou shalt be saved (Acts 16:31, KJV). Not, "join the church." The church did not die for the sins of the world. It was the precious

Lamb of God that died. Moreover, "He that hath the Son hath life" (1 John 5:12, KJV), not, "He that hath the church." The wages of sin is death, but the gift of God is eternal life through Jesus Christ. The gift of eternal life came by way of Christ, not the church.

Putting it rather bluntly, will your conversion experience take you to Heaven? Or, are you in doubt? The Lord Jesus Christ alone can save you. The church is but the instrument in God's hands.

Thirdly, did old things pass away and all things become new? I heartily believe that these searching questions will enable us to get our spiritual bearings. And, if you really accepted Jesus Christ, then 2 Corinthians 5:17 should and must be progressively manifested in your life.

Therefore if any man be in Christ, he is a new creature: old things are passed away; behold, all things are become new.

2 Corinthians 5:17 (KJV)

Paraphrasing, Paul means if you have not at least begun to hate the things you once loved and love the things you once despised, I am forced by both my Bible and experience to doubt your salvation. If you still desire and condone sin in your life and still hanker after the ways of the flesh, I would sincerely interrogate your spiritual experience.

Consider the oak tree. The old leaves represent your sins which have clung onto you through the bleak winter of your life without Christ. But then, spring arrives, budding and throbbing, pregnant and with new life it takes place in your heart, and your sins, like dead leaves, will gradually be pushed out of your heart and life.

Now, in closing, I would bring a few marks that distinguish the saved from the lost. We will seek to reestablish the line of demarcation so that each may know where they stand with God. These evidences are several, and may the Lord help us to examine ourselves by them.

To begin with, the truly born again enjoy a new walk. Yes, those who have experienced the saving work of God in being born again will enjoy a new walk before both God and man. "Whosoever is born of God does not commit sin" (1 John 3:9, KJV). The translation of "commit" in your Bible translates the verb "practice." The saved do not practice nor condone sin.

Love not the world, neither the things that are in the world. If any man love the world, the love of the Father is not in him.

1 John 2:15 (KJV)

Listen once again, "Whosoever abides in him sinneth not." The child of God abides in God. They enjoy a new walk. Is this your experience? Examine yourselves.

The truly born again will manifest a new affection. Those who are saved and have the Spirit of God dwelling in them will progressively manifest a new affection for the things of God. May I remind you that I am speaking of the born again children of God? Compare them to the many cold, formal, and heartless church members who have nothing but an empty profession.

111

This new affection will be manifested in several ways. Jesus will become increasingly precious to you. Yes, you will love Him, worship Him, adore Him, and serve Him. Your entire life will be influenced by Him. Is He truly precious to you or is He more abstract than real?

Also, the Bible will be cherished by you. To the saved, or the Bible Christian, the Bible is loved and read. The Bible is not just a book. It is the Living Word of God, and if you don't like to read it, there's something wrong with your spiritual experience. The Bible has character, personality, and life. It is the written Word of God.

Prayer will be an unspeakable delight. To the saved, prayer is not a mere duty to be performed, neither drudgery to be endured, but it is an unspeakable delight. If you don't enjoy praying, there's something wrong with your spiritual experience. Think of this! Who would not enjoy talking to God in prayer? Professing Christian, if you have no desire to get alone with God in prayer, I would certainly examine my experience and see if I'm in the faith, or just living a sham.

Christian fellowship will be a joy.

We know that we have passed from death unto life, because we love the brethren.

1 John 3:14 (KJV)

Do you love to fellowship with true Christians? Or are you more at home in a card game, or on the dance floor, or in the theater? We are talking plainly here. This is no time for mincing words. There is too much at stake. Examine yourselves, whether you feel at home with the people of God or like a fish out of water.

Your heart's interest will be in Heaven. We will not place our confidence in the passing things of life, but in the life that is to come. Is Heaven real to you? Are you looking forward to its blessings, its splendor, the meeting of loved ones and friends? You will not drive your stakes too deeply into this old earth if Heaven is real to you. But, sad to say, millions of people live and die without ever discovering this land of Heaven. It remains as unknown to them as the second stanza of "The Star-Spangled Banner."

The story is told of a rich plantation owner who died and, after the funeral service, his uncle returned to the home of the deceased. While there, the uncle asked the hired hand, "Joe, do you think your boss went to Heaven?" The hired hand replied, "When my boss used to go to Memphis, he talked about Memphis before he went, and he talked about Memphis a long time before he made plans to go, but I've never heard my boss talk about Heaven. I guess he never went there."

Where is your heart's interest? Does your life bear these several marks of conversion? If you are not able to give a clear-cut testimony of salvation in your life, then please don't waste another moment not knowing Him. May the Spirit of God strive with us. Tonight, let us fall at the feet of the One who loved us with an everlasting love and gave Himself for you on Calvary's cruel cross. There is hope in none other:

And she shall bring forth a son, and thou shalt call his name JESUS: for he shall save his people from their sins.

Matthew 1:21 (KJV)

Paul exhorted the Philippian jailer:

And they said, Believe on the Lord Jesus Christ, and thou shalt be saved, and thy house.

Acts 16:3 (KJV)

Jesus Himself tenderly entreats you tonight:

Behold, I stand at the door, and knock: if any man hear my voice, and open the door, I will come in to him, and will sup with him, and he with me.

Revelation 3:20 (KJV)

Will you not, sinner friend, you who are hesitant about your salvation, you who are in doubt, reply to the Spirit's pleadings in the words of this song that has a tender appeal:

> *I hear Thy welcome voice*
> *That calls me, Lord, to Thee,*
> *For cleansing in Thy precious blood*
> *That flowed on Calvary.*
>
> *I am coming, Lord,*
> *Coming now to Thee!*
> *Wash me, cleanse me in the blood*
> *That flowed on Calvary.*

("I Hear Thy Welcome Voice" by Lewis Hartsough, 1872. Public Domain.)

Chapter Nine

THE DEDICATION

For now I have chosen and consecrated this house that My name may be there forever, and My eyes and My heart will be there perpetually.

2 Chronicles 7:16 (NASB)

Keith and Mary Williams had no shortage of testimonies when it came to ministry. Ministry was their life, and they lived and breathed it so vibrantly. Now almost seventy years after Keith's ordination by Kathryn Kuhlman, I found myself the eager recipient of the church history pouring out of them. Divine appointments occur around us constantly and can be enjoyed by simply opening our eyes and looking for them. Such an appointment was taking place in 2007, right before my very eyes, in that humble home in Watertown, South Dakota.

Here was a couple that was almost giddy. It was like their memories had been frozen in time for the past seven decades, waiting to be thawed by my many questions. I laughed out loud as they would interrupt one another and add to one another's statements, constantly building and developing the narrative. As the hours passed, the storyline took shape. The skeleton of a timeline I had created from newspaper articles and history books began to take on muscle and flesh. Segments of time unaccounted for began to fill in and questions about the past began to dissolve.

An obvious thread to everything Keith and Mary shared that day was how incredibly much they enjoyed their season at Radio Chapel while serving alongside Burroughs and Kathryn. Mary shared from a grateful heart, "We did enjoy our ministry there, and the Lord blessed us and blessed those who came. We saw many, many, many people come to know Jesus as their personal Savior, and that was the only reason that I planned to be there or anywhere else. We all had our parts to play while we were there. We enjoyed it."

Preaching and declaring the Word was of the utmost importance to the preaching team at Radio Chapel. In fact, services were viewed as much more than meetings. They were events. The distance that people would travel to participate in the services was amazing and demonstrated the popularity of Radio Chapel. Keith shared that it wasn't uncommon to see people from Minnesota, Illinois, Missouri, Nebraska, and the Dakotas. He also stated that families would travel from Canada, as well as Kathryn's church in Colorado, to attend evangelistic crusades. People were fascinated with both the modern-day vision and futuristic design of Radio Chapel.

"The building was gorgeous and it had gorgeous wood beams," Keith proudly shared. "We had a disappearing pulpit and the lighting behind the pulpit was like stars in the sky. The choir platform could be raised up and down too, and you could hear the choir begin to sing before the platform was raised. We put the organ and the piano on either side of the choir."

Mary continued, "The music sounded so good in there with all those pipes and things on the organ. When that started up, you could just feel the vibration. The music was very worshipful. At the beginning, the people were pretty skeptical, you know, but I think they got pretty proud of everything when they saw how it was coming out."

"Every night we had a full house," Keith added. "Over 500 people every night, and our church was packed out for our revivals." There was a good reason for a full house. Radio Chapel was conducting an ongoing evangelistic campaign, something that hadn't been experienced or even attempted by many people. Whereas a typical tent revival might last weeks or even months, the vision at Radio Chapel was designed to encompass years. Keith referred to Radio Chapel's purpose as "soul-saving evangelism" that was sustained by "compassion for those who still needed the Lord." This was Burroughs and Kathryn's approach to ministry, and they didn't consider ministry successful until people were saved and changed.

"When the dedication was held," Keith said, "they couldn't get all the people inside. One of the messages preached that week was, "Upon This Rock I Will Build My Church." That was a busy time for all of us, but it was a privilege as well." Radio Chapel was only celebrating its first anniversary, but so much had been achieved. Whether it was outreaches to the surrounding communities, daily radio broadcasts, or the bi-monthly ministry magazine, there was still no shortage of work to be done.

Yet, it didn't feel like work to Mary. "Burroughs and Kathryn could touch people's lives like nobody's business. And the devil knew that. It was so peaceful and wonderful. It didn't feel like we needed anything else except their preaching." Mary became quite emotional while sharing her memories of those times. The intensity and power of those years at Radio Chapel made an indelible mark on her soul, greatly impacting her life and ministry as well.

The Mason City *Globe Gazette* published thirteen separate articles between July 9 and July 21, 1938, covering the events surrounding the dedication of Radio Chapel. The dedication was scheduled for Sunday, July 17, with a citywide parade to be held on Saturday, July 16. Services were suspended for the week prior to the dedication in order to allow for the completion of the Chapel's interior.

Radio Chapel was one of America's first media covered megachurches of the Twentieth Century. It seemed that local and regional media reported about every meeting, program, and project. Dozens of newspapers, some as far away as Detroit, Milwaukee, and Kansas City reported regularly on the happenings at Radio Chapel. And the popularity of the "Louisiana Pulpiteer" and the "Girl Evangelist" only fueled the media coverage. It was not unusual for families to drive two hundred miles or more to have the opportunity to sit under Kathryn's ministry.

The construction of Radio Chapel was being finished at the same time plans were being carried out for the dedication ceremony. It was daunting to say the least. During the suspension of meetings the week prior to the dedication, workers were rushing to complete the addition of the front of the facility's structure and various installations in the main auditorium. The grounds surrounding the Chapel had been landscaped and a baked enamel sign with neon lighting was to soon be installed.

"The Most Unique Church in the World" was an affectionate nickname given to Radio Chapel from its inception, and the church's amenities surely lived up to its title. Engineers had installed a year-round air-conditioning system that was claimed to be "the finest that modern science has been able to devise." Specially designed blue and silver opera chairs from the American Seating Company were scheduled for installation in the auditorium just days before the dedication. A new Steinway grand piano that was finished in ivory was delivered during the week, and the Chapel's Hammond Electric organ had been finished to match the new piano. Office furniture, carpet, linoleum, and the electronically operated blue curtain to be suspended in front of the large choir loft were also purchased. The tile work for the foyer and the acoustical work in the auditorium were being done under the supervision of an acoustical engineer. Lastly, an elaborate indirect lighting system was being installed just prior to the big celebration. Assurances were regularly given that the building would be finished just in time for the dedication service.

The Radio Chapel monthly magazine arrived in mailboxes with an article highlighting the short history, the ongoing purpose, and the upcoming dedication of the Chapel:

The House that God Built

God answers prayer! Dear Gospel partners, by His grace and your cooperation and sacrifice, it seems now that one of the most cherished dreams of my life will come true: the dedication of Radio Chapel on July 17, 1938, just one year to a day from the first service of our independent revival campaign in Mason City.

It is with the sincerest feeling of gratitude to our Lord and to you that I look forward to the completion of "The Most Unique Church in the World." It is my heart's firm resolve that Radio Chapel shall be used constantly to forward the Kingdom of our Christ in the salvation of souls and the establishment of His Own in the Word.

Matthew 21:13 says, "And said unto them, It is written, My house shall be called a house of prayer." Radio Chapel will be known throughout the nation for its many modern innovations. Thousands will no doubt be interested in the bright, attractive auditorium with its great rainbow arches, indirect lighting features, song screen, disappearing pulpit, unique choir arrangement, the beautiful chairs, and unusual color designs. But it will not be to all these things that our visitor's attention will be first called. As he nears the entrance of the finished Radio Chapel, his attention will be arrested by the inscription on the marquee, "The House that God Built."

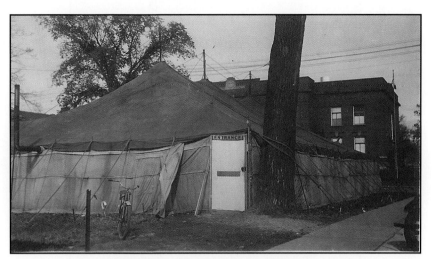

Radio Chapel Revival Tent

Radio Chapel Revival Tent with
Burroughs Waltrip

Guest Evangelistic Party will appear Sunday March 20th

Miss Kathryn Kuhlman, founder and director of the Denver Gospel Tabernacle, Denver, Colorado, and recognized as one of America's outstanding young lady evangelists, will begin a series of meetings at Radio Chapel Sunday, March 20. Miss Kuhlman has held meetings in the leading Gospel centers of the country, and has drawn tens of thousands by her unusual style of preaching and fine messages.

Miss Kuhlman has had no special training, as a child she felt led of the Lord to enter the evangelistic field and began holding independent meetings finally she held a meeting in Denver, Colorado which was so sucessful and stirring, that she was asked to build an independent non-denominational Gospel work. She has what is considered one of the finest Young Peoples works in the United States. Miss Kuhlman has a most unusual platform personality and this, coupled with her ability as a preacher, easily makes her the greatest young lady preacher in America.

Assisting Miss Kuhlman in her meetings in Radio Chapel will be Miss Helen Gulliford, and Mr. Harry D. Clarke. Miss Gulliford accomplished pianist, and song composer of the Denver Tabernacle, is considered one of America's finest Gospel pianists.

Harry D. Clarke, founder and director of Clarke's Tabernacle in Waterloo, Iowa, will be in charge of the choir work and congregational singing during their campaign. Mr. Clarke was a song leader for "Billy" Sunday, noted Evangelist. Therefore we feel Mr. Clarke is well known throughout the country for his ability as a song leader as well as an Evangelist.

"We are indeed fortunate in having this talanted evangelist party at Radio Chapel at this time, and we feel that this will be a turning point in evangelism in this section of the country. We are expecting hundreds of souls to be won during this campaign," stated Mr Waltrip.

Radio Chapel Magazine article about Kathryn

Newspaper advertisement for one of Kathryn's campaigns

Burroughs Waltrip breaking ground for
Radio Chapel Church

Radio Chapel construction with Revival Tent
in the background and Burroughs looking on

Radio Chapel Exterior

Radio Chapel Interior

Radio Chapel Dedication Week

Kathryn Kuhlman service at Radio Chapel

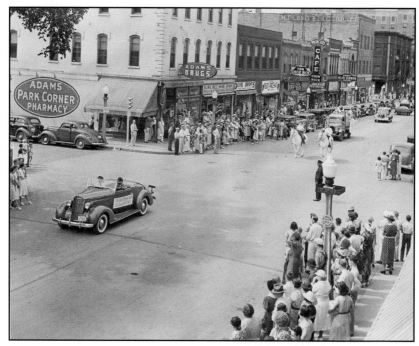

Radio Chapel Dedication Parade with Burroughs
in the lead vehicle

Radio Chapel Dedication Parade with Kathryn
in the vehicle with billboards

Keith and Mary Williams ordination service conducted by
Burroughs Waltrip and Kathryn Kuhlman

Burroughs and Kathryn presenting a Bible and
certificate of ordination to Keith Williams

Postcard from Waltrip and Kuhlman

Radio Chapel banquet with Kathryn, fifth from the left, and
Burroughs, sixth from the left, standing at the head table

Since its inception last summer in the revival campaign which gave birth to it, Radio Chapel has been subject to God's leadership and blessing in answer to prayer. Marvelous things have been done; unbelievable progress has been made. When one thinks that just last July 28, the very first service was held without local sponsorship and without external backing, and that today, the great auditorium of the Chapel is nearing completion, he feels like stopping in the midst of his labor and looking up long enough to say, "Thank God for answered prayer."

There is no membership in Radio Chapel. There will be none. The work is entirely independent of a superior governing body. It is purely undenominational. Its board of directors are chosen from all churches without regard for such affiliation or lack of it. And yet, with all its independence, it is entirely and completely dependent on God. It must always, as it has from the beginning, look to Him for its sustenance and continued success.

Since prayer is so essential to its progress, its very life, there must constantly be a spirit in the work conducive to prayer. And not only must there be much prayer, it must be the prayer of faith. Everything depends on that. The spirit of prayer must be safeguarded against every hindrance to a depth of consecration that is so imperative in real prayer life.

A spirit of one accord must prevail among those into whose hearts God has put the burden and whose eyes have caught the vision of Radio Chapel. In spite of the fact that there is no membership in the work and therefore no personal obligation or responsibility, there are many precious saints of God upon whom God has placed the anointing of faith and called to a fellowship of prayer. That fellowship must be held as sacred. Nothing must be allowed to break it down. To see that spirit of unity destroyed will be to glimpse the wreckage of the greatest call to get out of traditional ruts that this generation has yet heard. That spirit, the spirit of one accord, must be and will be preserved.

Prayer only gets real results when it is voiced from a heart truly humble before God. One with a bitter, critical, and judging heart is never a prayer warrior. His vision is blurred. His sensitivity is dulled. He cannot hear the tender Voice for his own pratings. His heart must be humble. And that doesn't mean that God is satisfied with that kind of humility that boasts of itself. That is not humility. It is rank pride of the worst kind. God blesses that humility that says, "Lord, I am not worthy of the least of Thy blessings, but in Jesus' Name I pray."

The prayer that will honor God and more than justify our faith in Him is that prayer that is backed up with works. God, indeed, wants us to have grace for obedience unto faith. If our prayers are backed by a spirit of sacrifice, a spirit of obedience, then God can and will do mighty things for us, to us, and through us.

Let every friend of Radio Chapel and its great evangelistic ministry wait on God for a vision of what God is wanting to accomplish through "the most unique church in the world," and then, having caught the vision, take the burden of prayer and touch God in simple faith for the glories He is more than willing to give. Make Radio Chapel a house of prayer by believing God for its completion, just as He would have it. Make it a house of prayer by praying daily for God's anointing upon its services. Make it a house of prayer by entering its doors ever in the spirit of prayer. It will be "The House that God Built."

Please continue to pray; attend every service possible; and remember to tell everybody that God answers prayer because of Calvary.

A massive parade was scheduled for Saturday afternoon, July 16, and would include forty decorated cars, twenty floats, and several groups from Radio Chapel, augmented by a local junior drum and bugle corps. The parade march was set to take them through Mason City's principal streets. The parade was advertised as the beginning of a full week's series of dedication and first anniversary programs. "This has in many respects been the most wonderful year of my life," Burroughs stated. "It is the first time in my ministry that I have ever felt that I was building something in which I was to have a permanent part. The parade is a kind of triumphal march. There have been numberless obstacles encountered in the building of Radio Chapel, but the Lord has never failed me, and hundreds of faithful friends have stood loyally by. I want Mason City and North Iowa to enjoy this victory with me. This is my home now and as nearly as I possibly can, I want to benefit this great community with my working here."

Burroughs felt that competition from the radio and the amusement world had caused the modern evangelist to change their tactics and the modern evangelistic effort would need to be sustained and continuous rather than occasional. This marked one of the important reasons for the establishment of Radio Chapel as an independent evangelistic center in Mason City. He stated that while Radio Chapel was now a permanent institution, its field was different from the other religious organizations of the community and it differed from the other churches of the city in that it had no membership. In summary, Burroughs firmly believed that there was the same Scriptural authority for the establishment of a permanent evangelistic center as there was for conducting a short series of revival services.

Margaret Quick Armstrong, a local contributing reporter, penned an article that ran in the *Globe Gazette* the week prior to the parade and dedication. In it, she praised the energy and efforts of all involved in the vision and construction of Radio Chapel, even sharing excerpts from a recent service:

> There was a large audience in attendance, and simultaneously with the first majestic notes of "The Star Spangled Banner," played as a prelude by Mr. John, they rose and stood very reverently at attention, after which Mr. Waltrip offered prayer. Then just before the sermon, the subject of which was "The Red, White, and Blue," the audience joined enthusiastically in singing "America," accompanied by the deep tones of the organ and its silvery chimes.

> It was a masterpiece, that sermon, spoken with such earnest fervor as is all too seldom heard. Mr. Waltrip opened his remarks by giving a very splendid eulogy to the Red, the White, and the Blue, saying next to the flag of his Lord, it was precious to him, and was the most beautiful flag in all the world today.

> The RED—may it never stand for the Godless red of communism, but for Christian courage, and hope—it could

stand for the priceless Blood of the Savior that washes whiter than snow.

The WHITE—has never meant "surrender" in the annals of America, never stood for cowardice either mental or physical. It has always stood for purity of life and purpose, and could stand for our redemption through our Savior Jesus Christ.

The BLUE—represents the perfect color in the Scriptures, and always stands for Truth, and integrity, and the cardinal virtues of honesty, and should stand for righteousness in the hearts of the American people.

The gist of the sermon was our debt of gratitude and praise and thanksgiving to God for His wonderful beneficence, His many blessings to us as a nation, and the thought that the continuance of these blessings must of necessity depend on our acknowledgement and appreciation of them. Mr. Waltrip said he was thankful to Almighty God that the pendulum seems to be swinging back to the religious principles which were the integral life of those who, by the Grace of God, founded America on the fundamentals of freedom—"life, liberty, and the pursuit of happiness," the only basis for true Americanism. Those who are destroying faith in God are undermining the very foundations of American liberty and courting ghastly disaster for their home and country. A Christian nation true to God need not fear disaster. The thing he most feared was not Communism, was not Nazi influence, was not fascism, but the apostasy found in the American pulpits.

The downfall of all nations in the history of the world has been preceded by a turning away from God; and the same cause will produce identical results today. The healing of our nation's ills will not be found in the political "isms" of our day, but as always, it will be found in a turning back to God and His providence.

"The House that God Built" was the name of the scheduled message to be preached at the dedicatory service. Burroughs said he had looked forward to speaking on this subject ever since he heard some of the flippant remarks of passersby while the foundation of the Chapel was being constructed early last fall.

Of particular interest was the fact that the Mason City Ministerial Association officially declined to take any part in the dedicatory services, and the president of the association stated he felt he could not speak at any of the services. Still, Burroughs extended a cordial invitation to all ministers of the community, as individuals, to be in any and all of the services. Burroughs stated that he did not feel that he was a competitor of other ministers, but rather that all were engaged in a common enterprise for the spiritual and moral betterment of the community. The stress between Burroughs and other local ministers was starting to show more acutely as pastors began to distance themselves from the efforts of Radio Chapel.

Dedication week was kicked off on Saturday afternoon with a parade route nearly one mile in length. The crowd, estimated to be at least three thousand in size, witnessed the parade of sixty-five decorated floats, private cars festooned with decorations and signage, and musical organizations from throughout the area.

126

Keith and Mary rode white horses supplied by Mary's father for the celebratory parade, while Burroughs rode in a 1937 Packard 110 convertible coupe with a sign on the door that read, "The old time religion is always up to date." When I asked Mary if Kathryn wanted to ride a horse, she politely folded her hands and smiled. "Kathryn was not about to get up on a horse. That just wasn't her style." Mary said that Kathryn instead rode in one of the enclosed cars, a 1937 Plymouth coupe, as the sun was very intense on that hot July day.

The dedication service held on Sunday, July 17, 1938, launched a week of special services and evangelistic messages designed in conjunction with the focus of the various nightly meetings. Radio Chapel was formally dedicated, climaxing the first year of the ministry's existence in Mason City. Capacity crowds made their way to the revival chapel daily. On Sunday evening, the message was titled, "One Year to A Day," and a birthday cake with one candle was placed upon the podium for the occasion.

Monday evening consisted of an Open House, at which the crowd was estimated to be between fifteen hundred and two thousand people. "Hosts and hostesses were on hand to explain and demonstrate the unique features of the building and its equipment. For more than three hours, the indirect lighting system, the disappearing pulpit, and disappearing song screen were in constant operation. The Hammond electric organ and Steinway grand piano furnished a musical background during the evening," reported the Mason City *Globe Gazette*.

"Community Night" was observed on Tuesday evening in the series of dedication week services. A sizable audience heard the Rev. L. E. Wardle of Swaledale, who would later officiate at the marriage of Burroughs and Kathryn, speak Tuesday evening on "The Church of Christ in Community Life."

Wednesday evening was designated as "Mason City Night," where the guest speaker, Verne A. Mettler, a local attorney, spoke on the subject of "Visions, Convictions and Courage."

Thursday evening was designated as "State Night," where the thrust of the message was geared toward spiritual values, vision, conviction, and courage.

Friday evening, "Young People's Night," was the scene of a thirty-minute drama entitled, *A Living Sermon*, which was produced and directed by Mary.

Finishing the week with "Commitment Night," was none other than Kathryn Kuhlman. There could have not been a more qualified speaker to speak on the subject of commitment, as Kathryn lived and breathed that quality in both her personal life and ministry. Reflecting back upon the splendor of that dedication week, Mary thoughtfully shared, "We were in the midst of it all! It all started out so beautiful. We were amazed it all happened so quickly. We did enjoy it. We enjoyed every bit of it. Radio Chapel was an unusual situation. The church and everything about it was different, so different. The people just couldn't wait until the building got done."

Kathryn realized the importance and weight of their accomplishment. This was not a light thing that had been achieved in such a remarkably short time in Mason City. She also believed in changing lives, but knew that ultimately it was God Who did the work of change in a person's heart. As a result, her messages were carefully crafted to speak to the needs and hearts of her hearers. All of her sermons were prudently titled to precisely reflect the content of the message. Over fifty sermon titles that Kathryn preached during her time at Radio Chapel were published in the *Globe Gazette* over the course of two years. "God and the Scissors," "You Can't Take it With You," and "Gone the Stain" are examples of just a few. She would also preach a series of messages such as "Outline of Faith," "Outline of Love," "Outline of Christian Living," and "Outline of Victory."

Seizing the opportunity to drive home the necessity of Christian longevity and commitment, she preached a brief, yet powerful message on the importance of walking with God. Her message was titled, "And Enoch Walked with God."

And Enoch Walked with God

Our text found in Genesis 5:24 says, "And Enoch walked with God: and he was not; for God took him." If evangelical Christianity is to stay alive, she must have men again, men who walk with God. She must have the stuff prophets and martyrs are made of. The newspapers in our modern world need to insert on the want-ad page: WANTED TODAY: MEN AND WOMEN, YOUNG AND OLD, WHO WILL OPEN UP THEIR HEARTS AND OBEY THEIR CONVICTIONS, EVEN IF AT THE COST OF FORTUNE AND FRIENDS AND LIFE ITSELF.

What a statement, "Enoch walked with God." The name "Enoch" means, "disciplined, yielded, and well regulated."

It is no wonder the writer could say he walked with God. In studying the life of Enoch, let us take a few simple truths to assist our memory.

First, regard his commencement. He began and he walked with God. Enoch was not a great man like Abraham, Joseph, Moses, David, Daniel, Elijah, or Paul. He was not a statesman, warrior, orator, or scholar. He was great because he walked with God. He practiced the presence of God in his life. He walked in the present tense. Enoch was a rare soul.

The commencement of Enoch's walk with God was known to him and was definite. He knew that he was walking with God. Enoch, while others were at variance with God, walked against the current of public opinion. He braved the current of men's minds.

Second, Enoch's walk with God was congenial. It was perfect harmony. There was no clashing. Walking with God makes life joyful and full of gladness. Dr. Webster tells us that to be congenial is to be, "kindred in spirit, agree-able, compatible, capable of existing together in harmony and not being antagonistic." Enoch walked with God in congeniality.

Third, in Enoch's walk with God, there was companion-ship. What question does Amos ask in Amos 3:3? "Can two walk together, except they be agreed?" In other words, there must be companionship and understanding. The Hebrew word for "walk" as used in the text means to walk continually up and down with God in both prosperity and in adversity.

Enoch and God walked as companions. To Enoch, God was an everlasting present and personal God as they walked in companionship. But notice, it was a mutual companionship. Enoch walked with God, but at the same time, God walked with Enoch.

One day, a pastor preached about Enoch walking with God, and a little girl went home and gave her version of Enoch walking with God. She told her mother, "One day, God went down to Enoch's house and got acquainted with him. Enoch was so happy that God came to see him that he said, 'I want to walk with You every day.' God said, 'Alright, come along.' So, every day Enoch went out to walk with God. They took each other by the hand and they enjoyed themselves. Then one day, Enoch forgot to look at his watch, and the sun went down, and the gates of Heaven were about to close. Then Enoch said, 'I'll have to spend the night in the woods.' But God said, 'Enoch, you are nearer to My house than you are to yours, come and go home with Me.' And Enoch said, 'Alright,' and he went. He liked it so good that he never came back." Enoch walked with God.

Chapter Ten

THE DEVIL'S DEMAND

**The thief cometh not, but for to steal, and to kill, and
to destroy.**

John 10:10 (KJV)

On Sunday, September 18, 1938, the *Waterloo Daily Courier*
published an article titled, "Court Inquires Into Man's Gifts
To Radio Chapel." Court hearings had begun in the town of
Hampton, which is thirty miles south of Mason City, regarding the
financial gifts of a 32-year-old oil dealer named Andrew Kaduce.
The newspaper reported that Andrew had given a $1,700 offering
toward the construction of Radio Chapel. Andrew's brother, George,
petitioned the court for the appointment of a temporary guardian for
Andrew, stating that he "has become unbalanced mentally because
of unsound religious fervor." Appearing before the judge, George
said that his brother, Andrew, had been attending services at Radio

Chapel and had recently attempted to borrow $32,000 to pay off Radio Chapel's indebtedness.

A number of witnesses had been called to testify and share their insights regarding Andrew's "strange religious beliefs." Additionally, Burroughs had been subpoenaed for appearance at the hearing, but had been in Chicago throughout the week.

The next day, the *Waterloo Daily Courier* reported that the judge was expected to announce a ruling early in the week regarding the request for the appointment of the temporary guardian for Andrew Kaduce. "I want it understood that there will be no more donations made until there has been a ruling in this case," Judge Garfield told Andrew Kaduce late Saturday as a hearing of the case was ended, effectively freezing Andrew's offerings to his church.

Andrew was the only defense witness. Referring to Burroughs Waltrip, he said, "I would do anything for him and I'm sure he would do anything for me. There is a bond between us no one can separate." Burroughs' continued absence from Mason City prevented the service of a subpoena on him. The story began to rapidly unfold through a flurry of newspaper articles that were published over the next seven days.

Mason City Globe Gazette
September 19, 1938
Waltrip Announces Kaduce Will Attend Service Here

Burroughs A. Waltrip announced Sunday evening that he would present an explanation of the Kaduce guardianship action at the Radio Chapel service Tuesday evening.

His subject will be "A Crazy Man Gives a Gift," and he said that Andrew Kaduce, for whom a guardianship was asked last week in Franklin county district court on the grounds of mental incompetence, would be on the platform to give his testimony.

Mr. Waltrip also announced that on Monday night that he and his entire staff will present a program in the K. P. Hall at Hampton relating to the court action.

Judge T. G. Garfield announced Saturday that he would give his decision in the Kaduce case early this week. George Kaduce, Andrew's brother, brought the case because of alleged donations of sums totaling $1,700 to Radio Chapel by his brother, according to this petition.

Mason City Globe Gazette
Wednesday, September 21, 1938
Judge Declares Kaduce of Unsound Mind, Eccentric
Waltrip Believes Donor of $1,700 Knew Exactly
What He Was Doing

Judge T. G. Garfield delivered a verdict in district court in Hampton on Wednesday, finding Andrew Kaduce fit subject for a temporary guardianship in answer to a hearing held after the defendant's brother, George, had filed a petition asking for such a guardianship.

In his decision, Judge Garfield stated, "Andrew Kaduce is of unsound mind and eccentric." With consent of the defense attorney, J. E. Williams of Mason City, he appointed George Kaduce to the temporary guardianship. Attorney for the plaintiff was John Senneff, Jr., of Mason City.

The petition was filed after the defendant had donated approximately $1,700 to Radio Chapel of Mason City, and had allegedly wished to sell his Franklin county oil tank business to give the proceeds to the Chapel directed by Burroughs Waltrip.

Mr. Waltrip, contacted by the Globe Gazette in Mason City and apprised of the decision in the Kaduce case Wednesday, stated, "I am still convinced in my own mind that in my relationships with Mr. Kaduce these few times, that he knew what he was doing, why he was doing it, and was fully responsible for his actions.

"In any future action on Radio Chapel, we will endeavor to do the fair and right thing as we always have in the past," declared Mr. Waltrip.

In regard to refunding any money given to Radio Chapel, Mr. Waltrip said at his meeting in Mason City Tuesday night, that he would hold it until he was convinced that Mr. Kaduce was of unsound mind.

"If I was convinced this young man is not responsible, they wouldn't have to ask for it. I'd mortgage the building, or do anything to do the right thing. If I am convinced he is of sound mind, you've got a tough fight on your hands to get a cent out of me. Andrew Kaduce is of sound mind and he is happy he did it. I wouldn't sell my own convictions for $10,000,000."

Mason City Globe Gazette
Wednesday, September 21, 1938
Waltrip Strikes Back At Enemies of Chapel
in "Crazy Man" Sermon

Presents Kaduce "Not as a Martyr, but a Humble Child of God"

Preaching that "The Gospel of the Word of God is a record of sacrifice," Burroughs A. Waltrip, in his sermon "A Crazy Man Gives a Gift," at Radio Chapel Tuesday night, struck back at persons he believes were aiming at the Chapel and himself when action was started at Hampton last week to prove that Andrew Kaduce was of unsound mind when he gave $1,700 to the Chapel.

Judge T. G. Garfield delivered a verdict in district court at Hampton Wednesday morning, finding Mr. Kaduce a fit subject for temporary guardianship and stating that he found the defendant "of unsound mind and eccentric."

Mr. Waltrip presented Mr. Kaduce at the Chapel and allowed him to relate the story of his life, which had been given in court testimony. He was presented, according to Mr. Waltrip, "not as a martyr, but as a humble child of God who loves the Lord more than anyone else."

"If I was convinced this young man is not responsible, they wouldn't have to ask for the money. I'd mortgage the building or do anything to do the right thing. If I am convinced he is of unsound mind, you've got a tough fight on your hands to get a cent out of me.

"Andrew Kaduce is of sound mind and he is happy he did it. I wouldn't sell my own conviction for $10,000,000."

Mr. Kaduce stated he was born on a farm near Meservey, attended Alexander High School and Marquette University, studied electrical engineering, was employed *by the Wisconsin Telephone Company for a time and later returned to Iowa, where he started his own business at Hampton.*

During dedication week, he stated that he attended meetings at Radio Chapel and that three weeks ago he made up the balance needed in the collection to meet expenses of Radio Chapel at that time.

"The Lord lay the burden on my heart and I was willing to do it. Relatives found out the circumstances and I was summoned to appear at the Franklin County Court and was charged with being insane. And here I am," said Mr. Kaduce.

Mr. Waltrip dwelt on the theme that "it is easier for a camel to go through the eye of a needle than for a rich man to enter the Kingdom of Heaven."

When Mr. Waltrip reached the point in his sermon when he challenged that "Mason City's number one citizen won't be in Heaven, but that some of the people now thought to be little people would be Heaven's elect citizens," he took off his coat and started to preach.

"We are living in days of great spiritual conflict and you can rest assured that if any group starts out to work for the Lord that you will be maligned, abused, and adjudged. If you are trying to live for Jesus Christ, you have a battle on your hands.

"The devil may not stop your car, but you may find more than 10,000,000 times 10,000,000 devils in the swastika before Hitler gets through bluffing the world.

"That a man could be hauled before a judge on a charge that he is insane, because he gives to the Lord, shows how much we are in need of the old-time revival of religion.

"If a man comes to Mason City and stays true to God and refuses to bow down to ecclesiastical authority, though he may win more persons to Christ than all of them, he is frowned on.

"I'd rather rot in an insane asylum than be a free man in the most beautiful mansion in Iowa and go to Hell for it.

"The devil has garnered millions to be used fanning the flames of worldly pleasure. The people of God need to learn the meaning of sacrifice."

Mr. Waltrip said that this is a day when one has to "put cash on the barrel head." Materialization is in the hearts of men, according to Mr. Waltrip, who said, "The work of Jesus Christ means nothing. They are after the dollars and pennies. We have to meet our bills to be able to go on with this old-fashioned revival.

"I don't want to hear another yap out of anybody about giving money to the church of God as long as you allow men to go to a state owned liquor store and put down money for liquor.

"If you're looking for crazy people, take every man who puts money on the bookie at a 10-to-1 shot. Until you buzzards quit gambling and until you women quit playing bridge for money, don't talk to me about crazy men.

"If Mr. Kaduce had bought a new car with his $1,700, you would have said, 'What a lovely car Andrew has.' If he makes a deposit in Heaven—he's crazy.

"If Mr. Kaduce had invested in a business deal and let someone swat him—if he had been outwitted in a business deal like a lot of you smart birds—you would say 'tut-tut' and that would be all there is to it.

"Andrew Kaduce is out $1,700, but he's got a million in his heart. I would have a North Iowa editor give a bouquet to one of the few citizens who knows the need of this country for more places like Radio Chapel to preach the Word of Christ without any strings attached to it.

"Radio Chapel has accomplished more in one year than all of the churches with their hundreds of members.

"Let a businessman go broke and people will say 'too bad,' but let Burroughs A. Waltrip fail, and he's a 'liar, a crook, and everything else.'

"Nobody can say that Burroughs A. Waltrip has asked them for one red cent, but I have prayed all night and fasted for 13 days and 17 days. Every cent has been voluntarily given. The Bible is all I have, but I'm a millionaire.

"All of the natural backing of Radio Chapel is faith in God. Not one single individual has underwritten a single dollar. God's house is not yours or mine. And I'm not telling the financial condition of Radio Chapel, because it's nobody's business.

"Why should I tell? Nobody is going to take the responsibility. That information is held between the Lord and me.

The fellow who gets nosey is the first to cut your throat. If I told you how much I needed, it would stagger you.

"I have never made a statement that Radio Chapel is clear out of debt. We owe about $32,000 on air-conditioning equipment, seats, and outside equipment. But show me a building estimated at a value of $75,000 with only $32,000 still owed.

"Since my name has been drawn into this on the front pages of the newspapers, I don't take it lying down. This action was not aimed at Andrew Kaduce, but it was aimed at Burroughs A. Waltrip. It's the only way they can get at me.

"I am convinced that Mr. Kaduce is of sound mind. Mr. Kaduce doesn't want his money back. What am I to do? I don't have it. I couldn't give it back if I wanted to. Tonight, I don't have it in the bank to my name. The books are as clean as the First National Bank's—maybe cleaner. Radio Chapel is not afraid of a thing, if the truth is told about everything that is found.

"God answered my prayer. Do you think I'd take God's answer and throw it back in His face?

"This situation has made it extremely embarrassing for me. There are people who would rather tell a slimy tale on me than say, 'Waltrip is fair and square.' I am solely responsible for everything that goes on here. If it goes down, my name is mud. If it fails, I'm the goat. People know about this work for hundreds of miles. I feel that burden on my soul.

"I'm going to stay true to God, and keep on doing business at the same old stand."

Mason City Globe Gazette
Saturday, September 24, 1938
Waltrip Is Sued for $2,100
Recovery Of Gifts Asked
George Kaduce Files Action as Guardian for Brother, Andrew

A suit for approximately $2,100 was filed in district court here Saturday against Burroughs A. Waltrip and Radio Chapel corporation by George Kaduce, Hampton, as a temporary guardian of Andrew Kaduce, who recently was declared of unsound mind.

The petition asks for the recovery of alleged contributions by Andrew Kaduce to Radio Chapel and alleges that Kaduce "was led to believe that the contributions being made by him were in the interest of charity, whereas in truth and in fact the defendant, Burroughs A. Waltrip knew that the contributions being received from plaintiffs ward would inure to his own personal benefit."

The suit resulted from an order signed Friday by Judge Sherwood A. Clock at Hampton holding that "the best interests of Andrew Kaduce, a person of unsound mind, will be served by the commencement of an action against Burroughs A. Waltrip and Radio Chapel, to obtain restitution and repayment of alleged donations and contributions made by the said Andrew Kaduce to Burroughs A. Waltrip and the Radio Chapel at a time when he was of unsound mind and a spendthrift."

The court order also authorized the temporary guardian to employ the firm of Senneff, Bliss and Senneff to act as attorney in the prosecution of the action.

In connection with the assertion that Mr. Waltrip would derive personal benefit from the contributions, the petition pointed out that the lot on which Radio Chapel is built was purchased on a contract made by Mr. Waltrip personally.

The petition also asserts that the said lot will become the property of Mr. Waltrip when payments on the contract are completed and that it will not become the property of the Radio Chapel corporation.

Mr. Waltrip, when asked for a statement concerning the filing of the petition, replied:

"In pursuance with the policy of Radio Chapel's management of its business affairs, we have proven to several thousands of people in this section that our ministry and methods of finance are sound and above reproach and that their confidence is well grounded," the statement read.

"My attorney will at the proper time and place take pleasure in answering for me the accusations of the petition. In the meantime, my friends will continue to pray for and work with me in the salvation of every man and woman possible."

If the judge's surprise ruling that Andrew Kaduce was of an unsound mind due to religious fervor was shocking to the congregation at Radio Chapel, then the judgment of the lawsuit against them must have been doubly so. Andrew was a faithful and frequent attendee of Radio Chapel's services and was diligent to support the Chapel with his giving. However, according to Keith, many of Andrew's friends and business associates were members of the surrounding churches where attendance and finances had declined substantially as a result of Radio Chapel's growth. Burroughs clearly perceived this was an orchestrated attack on the ministry through backdoor methods.

"The Devil is very busy and we have to watch out," Keith said, looking me right in the eye. Keith and Mary were adamant that even though it was mere men who brought the attack against Radio Chapel, a person always needs to realize it is Satan who is at work behind the scene. Referring to Burroughs and Kathryn, Mary said, "There were a lot of people who began to feel they were shysters after that. It was such a shame what those people did to us."

Keith expressed that from that point on, it wasn't uncommon to overhear murmuring and criticizing amongst some in the congregation. "Remember, we had spies among us," he said, slowly shaking his head. Members from other churches began to infiltrate the services, gathering people to themselves in order to question the manner and methods of the ministry at Radio Chapel. Mary said they decided to "endeavor to walk in love" toward those who were troublemakers, but as soon as they would put one fire out, another would be started. Town leaders and prominent businessmen who had so heartedly embraced Radio Chapel since its inception, even sharing the platform with Burroughs and Kathryn at times, began the deadly duty of tale bearing. Keith shared in frustration that it felt like "the outside opposition we had when we were building the church decided to come inside."

The ministry team of Radio Chapel made a covenant amongst themselves to soldier on and continue preaching the Word in the face of the scowls and judgmental glances thrown their way. They felt strongly that what they were enduring was a supernatural assault of Satan, and that if they held true to their course and convictions, God would vindicate them in the end.

Although the newly dedicated facility felt fresh and new, there was a frustration and sadness that began to slowly permeate the church services. Daily it seemed, articles continued to pop up in newspapers throughout the region. People on the street no longer offered up congratulations for a job well done or a handshake in honor of Keith's recent ordination. Rather, Keith and Mary became the uncomfortable recipients of all types of probing questions.

"Where did all that money go?"

"Do you regret working for Radio Chapel?"

"Is the church really going to go under?"

"Didn't you know how hard it would be to keep something like that going?"

The vocal rebukes and doubts from the citizens of Mason City didn't make things any easier. Mary said that she and Keith, along with Burroughs and Kathryn, treasured their times of going out for coffee or a meal after services. Now those times of sweet fellowship became less frequent. "It affected everything," Mary said. "Before all of this happened, we didn't have enough seats for all the people to sit in. Now, all of the sudden, we can't get people to come to church."

Located inside the scrapbook that Keith gave to me was a poem which he had cut from a newspaper and pasted on one of the pages.

One day by chance, he came across the poem at the same time Radio Chapel was entering into that difficult season, and it served as a constant reminder of the destruction and sorrow that the damaging words and agendas of men can cause. The poem, *Busybodies*, was penned in the late 1800's by Elizabeth Buffum Chace.

Paul once wrote to Timothy, this truth he did declare
Of folks who went from house to house to peddle out their ware.
I think he called them busybodies, or something of the sort,
Or maybe it was "tattlers,"—just to make it short.

Among the Thessalonians, he found there quite a few
Who really walked disorderly, and were busybodies too;
Classed with thieves and murderers, Peter then declares
That they are busybodies in other men's affairs.

They tell me folk are different, times have changed you know;
I find there are busybodies just everywhere I go.
The preacher and his family have to bear the brunt
And the humiliation of the busybodies' stunt.

They talk about the preacher—he can't, to save his life,
Buy a piece of furniture, or a garment for his wife.
Without some busybody or tattler in the crowd
Gives out the information, "They're extravagant and proud."

The suit he chanced to purchase—the price was out of sight;
His hat and shoes too "nifty:" if he'd really done the right
He'd gone to Mrs. Tattler and asked for her advice.
She'd been so glad to give it, and settle on the price.

Then if the wife and children perchance get something new,
Why Mrs. Busybody just made the air turn blue.

"Where did they get the money to buy such lovely stuff?
My goodness, gracious, sister, their clothes were good enough."

What could we do without them—these busybodies? Say,
We'd have so little worry, we'd most forget to pray.
We wouldn't have a racket within the church domain;
The preacher and the people could live and dress the same.

I'm really thrilled about it, and will there ever be
A body of God's people so sanctified and free?
Whose words are golden apples in silver pictures rare –
They'd bring a blessing, and sunshine everywhere.

Chapter Eleven

KATHRYN KUHLMAN WALTRIP

What therefore God has joined together, let no man separate.

Mark 10:9 (NASB)

"We knew they were in love when they came to Mason City, and we also knew that Burroughs had been married before," Keith said, somewhat hesitantly, when our discussion eventually turned to the marriage of Burroughs and Kathryn. I instantly knew this was going be a difficult issue to discuss. Keith and Mary traveled alongside Burroughs and Kathryn for the entire Radio Chapel journey, through the good and the bad—from the beginning to the end. In addition to serving as their constant companions in ministry, they became Burroughs' and Kathryn's closest confidants. Along with the bond of ministry, there existed an equally resilient bond of friendship.

Burroughs had been married once before. He was wedded to Jessie Annabelle on December 12, 1926, in San Antonio, Texas. They had two sons, Burroughs Junior and William. Burroughs filed for divorce from Jessie on June 17, 1937, in the Marion County District Court of the State of Iowa, where at the time he lived as a resident of Knoxville. Paragraph IV of his divorce petition stated, "That since the marriage of plaintiff (Burroughs) and defendant (Jessie), the defendant has been guilty of cruel and inhuman treatment such as to endanger the life of the plaintiff. That she has threatened the plaintiff's life and has been guilty of other acts of cruelty." Furthermore, Burroughs requested that the court grant custody of the children to Jessie. He additionally agreed to provide monthly support to the best of his ability in whatever amount the court should deem proper and just.

The divorce decree dated June 29, 1937, reads, "The court on inspection of the record finds that the defendant, Jessie Annabelle Waltrip, has filed her written appearance herein and consents to the court's jurisdiction to hear and determine the matter, and that this court has jurisdiction of the parties and subject matter of this action. The court, having heard the testimony and being fully advised in the premises, finds that the equities are with the plaintiff and against the defendant, and that the allegations set forth in plaintiff's petition are true, and that the plaintiff is without fault in the premises.

"It is therefore ordered, adjudged and decreed by the Court that the plaintiff, B. A. Waltrip, be and is hereby granted an absolute divorce from the defendant, Jessie Annabelle Waltrip, and that the bonds of matrimony existing between plaintiff and defendant are hereby dissolved, terminated and held for naught."

When I asked Keith and Mary if Burroughs' prior marriage raised any eyebrows amongst the congregation, they looked at each other and simply shrugged. Keith stated that it really wasn't much of a topic that was discussed frequently and that most people simply knew there had been some sort of problem between Burroughs and Jessie that resulted in their divorce. "It wasn't the topic of conversation as I remember," Keith said rather bluntly. Additionally, neither Keith nor Mary had ever met or spoken with Jessie or Burroughs' sons.

Burroughs had proposed to Kathryn just a few weeks prior to their marriage, following his return from an evangelistic meeting in Chicago. Mary said, with a grin, that everyone knew it was just a matter of time before the two of them would end up in the altar for, "another reason besides preaching." The wedding ceremony was scheduled for Tuesday, October 18, 1938, following the evening service. Decorated invitations, rolled and tied to a white rose with a bow, were delivered by courier, inviting well-wishers to a reception following the ceremony to be held in the grand ballroom of the Hotel Hanford.

Burroughs' mother, Mrs. Lila Waltrip, traveled from Lake Charles, Louisiana, to participate in the wedding ceremony. The marriage certificate on file with the Clerk of District Court of Cerro Gordo County shows that Lila also served as a witness to the marriage. This was not Lila's first time in Mason City. The August 1938 edition of the Radio Chapel magazine published a piece regarding her recent trip to Mason City for the purpose of seeing the Chapel facility for the first time that her son had built. The second witness on the marriage certificate was Keith Williams, whom Burroughs had also requested to be his best man.

On Tuesday, the day of the wedding, the sanctuary at Radio Chapel was decorated following that evening's service. Bouquets of flowers and candles were quickly set in place as preparations were underway for the ceremony that was scheduled to take place shortly before midnight. A small group of friends and staff were present to witness the exchange of vows as many others made their way to the ballroom at the Hotel Hanford in order to attend the reception. According to Keith, Kathryn became lightheaded partway through the ceremony due to the stress of the moment and required a minute to sit in one of the chairs and regain her composure. After taking a moment to catch her breath, the wedding ceremony continued and ended right around midnight.

"It was proving to be a difficult time for all of us," Mary would later observe, "but doubly so for Kathryn. We could tell something had happened with her church in Denver before the wedding and then there were the problems we started having at Radio Chapel. All that, and the wedding, I think, was just too much for her to handle at once." Keith was also clear that the burdens of the Kaduce lawsuit and its ensuing financial struggles, coupled with increasing persecution from the city and region, was taking a toll on the entire Radio Chapel ministry team.

After finishing their vows and signing the marriage license, it was time to head to the very late reception down the street. The reception at the Hotel Hanford was a festive event. Mary shared that there were at least two or three cakes on hand, and that the ballroom had been decorated with streamers and confetti. The "grand" cake, as Mary referred to it, was "at least four to five tiers high and decorated with white and blue frosting." White was Kathryn's favorite color, while Burroughs' was blue. Over one hundred people attended the reception which began shortly after midnight, and photographers were on hand taking pictures of the festivities. Invited members of both the congregation and community visited the ballroom early into the morning, offering their congratulations and best wishes to the newlyweds. Various city leaders, as well as heads of business, especially those who felt they had a financial interest in Radio Chapel, also made an appearance in order to express their congratulations as well.

Keith shared that the telephone at the front desk rang constantly as calls came in from local and national friends of the ministry. It was very hard to get a moment with the bride or groom as they were continuously called to the telephone throughout the early morning hours of the celebration. "There was one call," Keith mentioned, "that upset Kathryn pretty good. It was a long distance call from Denver and the call lasted for quite some time. I remember it was from some of her people at her church back in Colorado, and she was on the telephone with them for almost an hour. It really upset her on the night of her wedding. I knew there were people there who didn't agree with her getting married and with what she was doing in Mason City. It was too bad they had to ruin that night for her." Keith paused, and then added, "Kathryn had done so well in Denver. It was her ministry, her word that built that church. She pioneered that work."

The reception ended at around 3 a.m. with plans for Burroughs and Kathryn to take some time away from Radio Chapel and their ministerial responsibilities to enjoy their honeymoon. They resumed preaching at the Chapel on November 1, with Burroughs' first message following the wedding titled, "Can A Saved Man be Lost" and Kathryn's first message back titled, "You Can't Take it with You." The Mason City *Globe Gazette* reported the wedding ceremony on the following day.

> Miss Kathryn Kuhlman, young blond evangelist who has assisted Burroughs A. Waltrip in campaigns at Radio Chapel from time to time the past year, was married to the Mason City "pulpiteer" at Radio Chapel at 11:30 on Tuesday night.
>
> A marriage license was obtained at the clerk's office in the courthouse Tuesday afternoon just before closing time. His age was given as 35 and Miss Kuhlman's as 24 years.
>
> The ceremony was a quiet one with only the immediate members of his staff present. The Rev. L. E. Wardle, pastor of the Methodist church at Swaledale, guest speaker at the dedication last July, performed the ceremony.
>
> Miss Kuhlman's address was given as Concordia, Missouri. For the past seven years, she has been engaged in evangelistic work. At the time she assisted in the local

Chapel campaign, she told of her own revival tabernacle at Denver.

Mr. Waltrip has been in Mason City 15 months conducting the Radio Chapel. He started preaching he said, when he was "only a kid," but has been at it steadily since he was 19 years of age.

Miss Kuhlman will now establish her headquarters in Mason City and assist Mr. Waltrip in the operation of Radio Chapel.

The marquee located above the front entrance of Radio Chapel was soon changed to reflect Kathryn's married name, "Kathryn Kuhlman Waltrip." The Mason City *Globe Gazette* followed suit and began referring to her in the newspaper as either "Kathryn Kuhlman Waltrip" or "Mrs. Burroughs A. Waltrip." Advertising for the Chapel changed accordingly as mailers, flyers, and handbills soon began introducing her by her new married name.

Kathryn's marriage to Burroughs and subsequent relocation of her ministry headquarters to Mason City, Iowa, was not well received by her church in Denver. As a result, Kathryn and the Denver congregation parted ways, yet she remained close friends with a number of the leaders of the Denver Revival Tabernacle for years to come. Mrs. Ina Fooks assisted Kathryn with her evangelistic work in Mason City, and Miss Lottie Anthony was in charge of the music department and financial business of the Chapel. Both women were associated with Kathryn in the operation of the Denver Revival Tabernacle.

Following their wedding, Burroughs and Kathryn conducted a number of evangelistic campaigns together, especially throughout the South. Both of them were well-known and highly regarded among their peers in the southern states and continued to enjoy wonderful meetings and warm reception with the people there. On four separate occasions over the next eight months, Radio Chapel's services were conducted by guest ministers, which allowed for Burroughs and Kathryn to conduct their meetings in other states.

It was a busy time for the Radio Chapel ministry team. In addition to conducting the daily services and radio broadcasts, there were the ever-present struggles that came as a result of pioneering a new and rapidly growing ministry, especially one that was under constant financial attack. Unfortunately, the wedding took place at the beginning of Radio Chapel's legal troubles, which didn't allow much time to rest for Burroughs and Kathryn.

Sharing the pulpit together, but now as husband and wife, was a new experience for both Burroughs and Kathryn. This was uncharted territory. The residents of Mason City and North Iowa were long familiar with the unique "preaching duo" at Radio Chapel. For the previous fifteen months, church attendees were accustomed to Burroughs and Kathryn ministering tag-team style and building upon one another's messages. With Kathryn in Mason City permanently following the marriage, it gave them an even greater opportunity to build upon each other's sermons and drive home the central truths of God's Word.

For example, on Sunday, November 20, 1938, Burroughs preached the message, "Saints and Robbers" at the 2:45 p.m. service and Kathryn preached the message, "You Can't Take It With You" at the 7:45 p.m. service. Two Sundays later, Burroughs' sermon was called, "A Banner In The Blood" and Kathryn's was titled, "Gone The Stain." In January, he launched the Sunday services with a message titled, "Jesus Christ and Company" which was followed up with Kathryn's message titled, "God's Red Light." On February 5, 1939, they changed up the order of speaking and Kathryn brought the morning message titled, "Our One Great Love" and Burroughs concluded the Sunday with the message, "On One Condition." Burroughs and Kathryn discovered this was an extremely popular and effective preaching method with people and they elected to follow the formula for months to come.

Keith and Mary loved to watch and hear Kathryn minister. She was both confident and comfortable in her own speaking ability, and her love for the Word of God and the presence of the Holy Spirit exuded from her at every service. Mary observed, "Kathryn was very dramatic and came out onto the stage sometimes almost like she was portraying an angel. She was very angelic-like. Kathryn was a beautiful woman and was precise in her appearance. She used to wear a white satin gown when she preached."

Both Keith and Mary felt it was an incredible honor sitting underneath Kathryn's preaching. They were especially fascinated with how enamored the people were with her ministry style. Mary said that Kathryn "had a little bit more soul" than other preachers, yet at times could lean toward the quiet side.

"She was very knowledgeable and sensitive to the Word," Mary added. "And she was great in praying. She spent a lot of time in prayer."

Keith continued, "The ministry was a big thing to Kathryn and very heavy on her heart when it came to prayer. Very heavy."

When I asked the both of them for their thoughts regarding how people further responded to Kathryn's distinct type of ministry, Mary said, "She would touch you and love you, and she was very dramatic while doing it. Most of the people had never experienced something like that." After pausing for a few seconds, Mary added, "There were many people who could see things in her. I don't really know how to explain it. It was a passion for the Holy Spirit."

Keith concluded, "It was an unusual situation. People couldn't wait until her services, and they were there for her whether it was summer or winter."

Chapter Twelve

THE SPIRIT OF SUSPICION

**For I am afraid that when I come I won't like what
I find, and you won't like my response. I am afraid that I
will find quarreling, jealousy, anger, selfishness, slander,
gossip, arrogance, and disorderly behavior.**

2 Corinthians 12:20 (NLT)

Dark clouds were gathering over Radio Chapel. The October 21,
1938 issue of the *Waterloo Daily Courier* reported that Andrew
Kaduce had filed a motion in the Franklin County District Court to
have the court set aside the previous ruling that stated he was of an
unsound mind and in need of a temporary guardian. Andrew, who
continued to attend services at Radio Chapel, contended that the
court had no jurisdiction to find him of unsound mind and that no
notice was given him of the order authorizing a suit against Radio
Chapel. He further contended that he had been unlawfully deprived
of his liberty and property. In early November, Andrew's efforts to

159

reverse the ruling against him were quickly overturned in the district court. The legal and financial woes of Radio Chapel were turning into an unstoppable juggernaut.

At the time of Andrew's failed motion, the lawsuit filed by his brother was still pending in the Cerro Gordo District Court to recover Andrew's donation. Attorneys for Burroughs and Radio Chapel conceded judgment for approximately $2,100 in the case in Mason City when Andrew was declared to be of an unsound mind, following the jury's verdict in the court in Hampton. Burroughs and his attorneys had previously agreed that, in the slim chance that Andrew was determined to be of an unsound mind, they would concede the case against the Chapel in Mason City. That hasty agreement proved to be unwise. The result was that neither Burroughs nor Radio Chapel would ever have the opportunity to argue their case in court, and further served to turn the tide of public opinion against the ministry. Additionally, the media-covered court proceedings fueled the hostility and criticism from local pastors who had lost members and finances to Radio Chapel.

"If I had the money back, I would give it again," Andrew said as his guardianship trial ended in Hampton. He also stated he would give more money, and additional money beyond that in the future if he saw fit. Andrew shared that his only interest was in helping pay off any debts at Radio Chapel. He also expressed the desire to follow a call from God to serve as an evangelist for Radio Chapel. Witnesses, many from surrounding churches, had been summoned to testify regarding the frequency of Andrew's church attendance and that he said that he wouldn't allow "the work of the Devil" to prevent him from attending services at his church. While the witnesses were being listened to, it was apparent that no one was listening to Andrew.

Attorneys for the plaintiff further stated in the district court proceedings a number of "factual allegations" regarding Andrew and Burroughs. First, they argued that "confidential relations existed between Andrew Kaduce and Burroughs Waltrip, and that Burroughs exercised undue influence upon Andrew and by trickery deceived him." Second, they stated that as a result of Andrew's offering, "Burroughs is guilty of fraud upon Andrew." Third, the attorneys stipulated that, "Burroughs exercised his dominant will upon Andrew." However, Andrew simply wanted to be able to give offerings to his church. Finally, the court's petition stated that, as a preacher, Burroughs is a person of strong personality and he exercised an undue influence over Andrew by the suggestion and promise of Heavenly rewards that led Andrew to give his offerings.

On November 18, 1938, the *Globe Gazette* reported that the Cerro Gordo County sheriff's office had received an execution of judgment against Burroughs Waltrip and Radio Chapel, which cleared the way for an officer of the court to take possession of the ministry's property. The seizure of the property was scheduled for later that day, and a notice of sale of the church facility was to be publically posted as well according to law. As a result of the extensive media coverage of the Kaduce case, a mechanic's lien was quickly filed at the clerk's office that same day by the Mason City Builders Supply Company for materials furnished in the construction of

Radio Chapel. The speed at which this methodical and coordinated assault was able to proceed was dizzying.

The following Sunday, Burroughs and Kathryn stood somberly before the congregation at Radio Chapel and presented a new fundraising effort. This fundraiser, however, was neither for construction nor for evangelism, but rather to satisfy the unexpected judgment against the church. Because Burroughs had previously said, "If Andrew is found to be incompetent of handling his business affairs and is adjudged of unsound mind, his money will be returned to him," he was now painted into a corner. There was no way around it. The judgment had to be satisfied. It was further shared with the church members that the sheriff had served a speedy execution on the judgments that called for the sale of the Chapel by December 19, 1938, unless the judgments were satisfied sooner.

Burroughs stated, "This is not a battle between flesh and blood, it is a spiritual battle. The devil is demanding the closing of Radio Chapel and the answer may as well be given now." He made an announcement to the public that he would raise the necessary money by freewill offerings from his congregation and said, "I believe that we will meet the challenge with great victory for the Lord in that the money will be raised in full by the set time of December 19." The congregation responded by immediately contributing $450 toward the approximately $2,100 needed funds.

Burroughs, Kathryn, and Keith steadfastly continued with the vision of evangelism at Radio Chapel. December began with a sermon preached by Keith titled, "When Life Begins" followed a week later with the aforementioned message brought by Burroughs called, "A Banner in Blood." The companion message to Burroughs was later preached by Kathryn and was titled, "Gone the Stain." Yet in the face of their optimism, the constant drumbeat of opposition and financial struggles continued to grow steadily louder.

"Again, we knew there were spies at every service," Keith sadly said to me. "We knew who they were and we knew why they were there. They were reporting back to other pastors in the town and to lawyers and government people. It was terrible seeing how cruel people could become when so much had been given to them like it was." Keith sat up straight and pointed his finger at me. "There's so much jealousy out there. People don't listen. They don't accept the truth."

Legal documents filed in the Kaduce case also later revealed that attorneys arguing against Radio Chapel had secured stenographers for the purpose of listening to the ministry's daily radio broadcasts. The documents further stated that the stenographers utilized the attorney's offices to take down the sermons in shorthand and transcribe those messages. It was further submitted to the court that their interest in the sermons was related to any of Burroughs' preaching about money or giving that might strengthen their case against Radio Chapel.

As December wore on, the snowball effect continued as more liens were filed almost daily against the Chapel by businesses that were fearful they would never see their money. By mid-December, liens and outstanding debts had mushroomed to more than $45,000 as a direct result of the extensive media publicity regarding the lawsuit and judgment against the ministry. Mary said that an understandable, yet unbearable, sense of desperation began to overtake the congregation while murmuring and second-guessing became increasingly prevalent.

DESPERATION SETS IN

With the original Kaduce judgment balance still hanging over Radio Chapel, Burroughs made an unexpected and unanticipated strategic decision in a risky attempt to save the ministry. As a result of the financial pressure, coupled with opposition from within and from without, he resigned as the director of Radio Chapel in order to "clear the decks" for a hopeful reorganization of the troubled ministry. Privately, Burroughs and Kathryn had informed Keith that their plan was to step aside to give both creditors and directors of the corporation the freedom needed to appropriately meet the impending crisis. Ministry supporters as well as others in the community were stunned by the sudden turn of events. How could a ministry with so much promise appear to be heading for complete disaster?

Keith announced Burroughs' sudden resignation on Tuesday, December 13, at the Chapel. He refused, however, to reveal any further information as to why Burroughs had resigned or to his whereabouts. Burroughs and Kathryn could not be reached at their apartment at the Hotel Hanford, having left at noon that day and not yet returned. The *Globe Gazette* and surrounding newspapers were quick to recount the history of Radio Chapel and the church's brutal financial woes. On Wednesday, December 14, the day following Burroughs resignation, the newspaper published a lengthy article highlighting an interview with Burroughs regarding the fast developing crisis.

Waltrip Quits As Director Of Radio Chapel

While the magnetic evangelist, Burroughs A. Waltrip, resigned director of Radio Chapel, was besieged by distressed friends eager to offer their suggestions in a time of crisis, lawyers were at work Wednesday, completing the transfer of his "house of dreams" to other hands.

Meanwhile Keith Williams, who not so many months ago was repairing tires and handling sales for a local super service station and who in the heyday of the Chapel operations was raised by Waltrip to the status of minister of the Gospel, found himself the head of a $75,000 corporation facing a financial crisis and possible complete disaster.

Pulpiteer Waltrip, while stepping aside to give creditors and directors of the corporation complete freedom to meet the crisis, which includes a scheduled sheriff's sale Monday at the courthouse, maintained emphatically that he was not "running away."

"I am staying here to help," he declared, banging a Hotel Hanford desk with a clenched fist. That was his answer, he maintained, to quiet rumors that he was leaving the city while his "dream chapel" was toppling on the brink of a financial abyss.

"People think I built that Chapel in a year," he said. "The fact is, I have been building that Chapel since I was 19 years of age when I started preaching. I am now 35."

His resignation was placed before the Chapel board, he said, in order to clear the decks for any reorganization that might restore the confidence of the community and meet the impending financial crisis of the $75,000 evangelistic center.

The immediate crisis is a sheriff's sale scheduled to take place Monday to satisfy a judgment of $2,044.54. In addition to this are other debts totaling more than $45,000, according to courthouse records.

"There have been no accusations, but to forestall any opinion that I am getting away with any money, I have asked my creditors to make an accounting of the Chapel receipts and disbursements as they have been kept by the treasurer, Mrs. Thelma Schweizer," Mr. Waltrip stated.

"At the present time I have $8 in a bank and an additional $125 between me and the end of the road, and at this time of the year, it is almost impossible to get evangelistic assignments. They will not become available before February.

"I am going to stay in Mason City and help all I can. There is nothing I need to run from. It is rather the other way around. I intend to make Mason City my permanent home. We want to show that we are 100 percent sincere and not financial racketeers. It is not my personal interests that are concerned. The question is whether I can save this, my boyhood dream."

There is a financial crisis, but no schisms in the work of the Chapel, the pulpiteer stated. "We have had more than 500 conversions since we started this institution," he said.

The building of his "dream chapel" was not a financial, but a religious venture, he added. "When I stopped here to organize this thing I canceled meetings for a year ahead throughout the Midwest," the evangelist stated. "I could have made a much larger salary doing that. The books will show that I have been paid a total of $4,000 for my salary and expenses here for 18 months. No one will say that is an excessive salary."

The Chapel fell into the present financial crisis because of his inability to finance the institution as planned, Mr. Waltrip explained. An application for a $32,000 government loan sent by the local representative of that agency was turned down.

"They will lend on a chicken coop, but not on a house of the Lord," he commented.

"If I had known that we couldn't be financed properly, I would not have gone ahead with the building of the front of the Chapel and the installation of seats," he said. "I had everything under control up to that point. Failing to get a loan, we had to turn to other sources and made the contract with Dr. E. E. Chappell to finance it. His inability to continue payments under the contract helped precipitate this crisis.

"It was not a case of Dr. Chappell's unwillingness but his inability to continue the payments and I released him.

"There may have been rumors that I would leave, but I have always said I won't leave without a parade and banners flying. I won't break faith with our friends. I want to do as nearly as possible what the good Lord and the community wants me to."

Mr. and Mrs. Waltrip's room at the Hotel Hanford has been besieged with telephone calls and personal visits since the announcement of his resignation. While a reporter was conversing with him, the hotel lobby porters were constantly bringing him phone calls and groups of visitors were waiting for an opportunity to see him.

"What's to be done to straighten this thing out?" he was asked.

"First of all, we must get rid of this spirit of suspicion that is evident in the community," he said. "I want to say that I have not been hounded by creditors. People who have filed liens have done so at my advice. I never knew businessmen could be so grand.

"The future will largely rest with our creditors and the ability to raise additional funds. The $2,044 judgment Monday is our first hurdle."

Although no longer the director of the Chapel, Mr. Waltrip attended the services held there Tuesday night when Evangelist Lamberson from Iowa Falls gave the sermon.

"I want to urge the friends of my ministry in Mason City to attend all services and to give all possible support," he said. "I intend to attend the services myself. I was there last night and for the first time realized how comfortable those seats are."

While attorneys were working on transferring Radio Chapel from Burroughs and Kathryn to the officers of the Chapel corporation, petitions were being circulated throughout Mason City asking the evangelist to stay in the city. "We the undersigned, friends of Burroughs A. Waltrip, in deep appreciation of his outstanding work here do herby petition him to remain in Mason City as our independent evangelist," was the wording of a petition that already had scores of names attached. The *Globe Gazette* reported that Burroughs reluctantly gave his consent to the circulation of the petitions, stating he would be glad to have the petitions circulated as a gesture of friendship. Burroughs further maintained that he was seeking to keep the Chapel membership from becoming a split. Additionally, a sixth mechanic's lien by the proprietor of a local paint store was added that day to the five previously on file.

It is always in the most difficult and darkest times that panic sets in. Even the most steeled man or woman of God can be shaken. In just eighteen months, Radio Chapel had gone from being the most celebrated religious story of the region to becoming the most besieged ministry of its day. It was of no surprise when cracks began to form in the leadership under the immense stress of the crisis. Unfortunately, virtually all of Radio Chapel's internal discussions and disagreements were quickly reported to the media by moles in the church just in time for the edition of the next day's newspaper, and on Monday, December 19, 1938, the *Globe Gazette* published an extensive write-up revealing the internal struggles and decisions of the church's leadership.

Reflecting back, Keith shook his head as he said, "Deacons and leaders at Radio Chapel were talking to the media and to legal people. We didn't know who was doing all the talking but it didn't help things at all. In fact, it made things worse." As a result of the increasing division and rifts between the remaining double-minded leadership, Burroughs reassumed control of the struggling ministry just six days after resigning and managed to raise an additional $1,000 toward the Kaduce judgment. These additional funds were able to delay the sale of Radio Chapel at the upcoming sheriff's sale. Andrew Kaduce continued to attend services at Radio Chapel in spite of the troubles surrounding the ministry as a result of his prior contributions, and was treated no differently by Burroughs, Kathryn, or Keith. The general attendance, however, had dramatically shrunk in size. Gone were the sweeter days of five hundred to seven hundred people regularly in attendance as the numbers had been halved to less than three hundred in less than six months.

The service held on Sunday, December 18, was difficult. Some of the listeners were moved to audible sobbing as they heard Burroughs' pleas to become "instruments of God" and help assist saving the church with their donations. The newspaper reported that shouts of "Amen" and "Hallelujah" greeted contributions. Kathryn, who only a few weeks earlier had become Mrs. Waltrip, sat on one side of the platform near the organ. "She sobbed almost constantly and hid her face in her handkerchief," Mary said, except when she was providing background exclamations for Burroughs' pleas, which centered on asking the people and businessmen to join the procession "for the good of the community to save the most unique church in the world."

That same Sunday following the evening service, many of the Chapel directors and leadership resigned as a result of the financial crisis that overshadowed the future of Radio Chapel. Some had been contacted by attorneys and were informed that the people who signed their names to any financial agreement in order to save the ministry would be held responsible not only as a corporation, but personally and individually as well for the debts of Radio Chapel. It was the straw that broke the camel's back for the majority of them, and they parted company with Burroughs and Kathryn right then and there.

Burroughs, in a desperate effort to right the ship, stated, "I am asking my creditors to form a committee to audit my records and to work with members of the corporation toward a systematic and early as possible liquidation of the indebtedness. This action has come because of the tremendous pressure of public opinion on my behalf and as an expression of confidence on the part of my creditors in my ability to keep faith with the community. I have faith in our cause in the face of the almost insurmountable financial obstacles that lie in our path. I want to express my sincerest appreciation for the confidence that has been shown me in this period of crisis. I am proud to have adopted Mason City as my home and I am confident that we are going to succeed."

The descent into the upheaval that followed was characterized by chaos and complete disorder. The *Waterloo Daily Courier* reported that Burroughs was "out and in again" as they referred to his resignation and subsequent decision to return as chairman of the "memberless" board. Statements were prepared and released to the media by former members of the board of directors as well as new members of the board. Many had secured the services of their own attorneys to protect their financial interests and liabilities with the corporation. In addition to the looming financial crisis due to judgments and liens, heated discussions began developing amongst the leadership regarding a plethora of issues such as the appointment of new board members, compensation plans, and logistical ministry agreements, in addition to an internal audit of the Chapel's financial records. Following a flurry of nonproductive meetings and with no resolution in sight, the remaining board members resigned leaving only Burroughs and Kathryn at the helm of Radio Chapel. "We the members of the board do not feel that we can be responsible for the $46,000 indebtedness on the Chapel, plus the $2,000 judgment," read a joint statement from the directors. "With the affairs in such a chaotic condition, we do not feel that the Lord would bless our efforts in trying to right the reeling vessel. For these reasons, we do hereby resign as officers of the board of directors of Radio Chapel, Incorporated."

Tragically, the rift claimed Keith and Mary as well. "I am no longer connected with Radio Chapel," the newspaper reported Keith as saying. "I want to express my sincere appreciation to the thousands of people in Mason City and all North Iowa for their confidence in my ministry."

Regrets

Sitting with Keith and Mary in their living room almost seventy years later following the occurrence of those events, I could feel the pain and regret in their voices. They both cried openly when sharing about the grief and sadness that surrounded the uncontrollable events of those days. It was obvious they wanted history to be much more kind to the efforts of those who sacrificed and suffered so much for the church called Radio Chapel. Keith wiped the tears from his eyes as he said, "The Devil was in all of that, and I know he was. It was the lawsuit that ended up forcing us out and that was a sad thing. We got attacked from all sides."

Mary made no effort to hide her tears. "There was so much debt," she said. "Before that, everything was at peace. We went through all of that, and it was not easy. It was true that Burroughs overdid things, and people eventually saw that, but it was a shame it happened like that. We just couldn't afford to pay for everything at once after the judgment. It really was a shame."

As both December and 1938 drew to a close, Radio Chapel was once again given a thirty-day breathing spell in which to work out the financial difficulties of the ministry in the form of a $500 cash payment towards the Kaduce judgment, staving off the sheriff's sale for a second time until January 25, 1939.

On December 31, 1938, the Mason City *Globe Gazette* published a comprehensive article detailing the year's events connected to Radio Chapel. The write-up, titled, "Radio Chapel in Headlines often in 1938," covered a wide range of topics.

Radio Chapel was one of the local institutions that helped make headlines during 1938. It started off the year in a new $70,000 building and with its founder and director, Burroughs A. Waltrip, holding services for audiences that often filled the auditorium in which 700 opera chairs with padded seats were installed prior to the midsummer dedication services.

The crowds continued to come throughout the spring and a two-story office addition was built on the front of the auditorium and a big colored neon sign erected on the corner of Pennsylvania Avenue and Second Street Northeast to advertise its presence.

Many of the listeners were first attracted by the evangelist's dynamic personality that reached out by way of daily radio broadcasts over station KGLO. Some perhaps came to see the building that he advertised as "the most unique church in the world."

It has no windows. Light comes from an indirect electric lighting system recessed in the walls and ventilation is provided by a year around air-conditioning system. No hymnals are needed. Hymn words are flashed on a disappearing song screen from an electric projector.

Furniture on the stage is finished in white, including the grand piano and electric pipe organ and a hydraulically controlled disappearing pulpit. Those accustomed to more conservative churches were inclined to gasp in amazement.

In February, Miss Kathryn Kuhlman of Denver was guest evangelist at Radio Chapel and assisted in the ordination of Keith M. Williams as assistant to Mr. Waltrip. Mr. Williams, a Mason City boy, before his connection with Radio Chapel had preached at evening services at Hanford while working during the day in a local tire shop.

Nine months later, Miss Kuhlman became Mrs. Waltrip and resigned as director of the chapel she had built in Denver.

In July, only a year after Mr. Waltrip's arrival in Mason City, Radio Chapel was dedicated, a feature of the week-long celebration being a parade through downtown Mason City.

As summer waned, the shadow of less fortunate happenings fell over the Louisiana Pulpiteer.

Suit was begun in district court at Hampton by George Kaduce to have his brother, Andrew, Alexander oil dealer, declared of unsound mind and to have a guardian appointed.

The trial brought out that he had contributed more than $2,000 to Radio Chapel and his brother feared that he would sell his business in order to turn over the proceeds to Mr. Waltrip to pay off the Chapel debt.

The courts eventually delivered a decision that Andrew was of unsound mind and a spendthrift and George was appointed guardian for his brother. The immediate result of his appointment was the filing of a $2,044 judgment in district court in Mason City against Mr. Waltrip and Radio Chapel.

Attorneys for George Kaduce and Mr. Waltrip had agreed previously that the judgment should be entered without contest if the guardian was appointed.

The date for the sheriff's sale of Radio Chapel to satisfy the judgment was set for Monday, Dec. 19. The preceding Tuesday, Mr. Waltrip's resignation was accepted by the board of directors of Radio Chapel who later revealed that "unreasonable" salary demands by the evangelist had caused the rift.

They reported that financial records of the Chapel showed more than $3,900 paid to Mr. Waltrip in salary and expenses during the previous 14 months and that their refusal to sign a 10-year contract presented by him calling for a starting salary of $75 weekly plus expenses precipitated his resignation.

Four days later, the three directors, Mr. Williams, Mrs. Thelma Schweizer, and Dr. E.E. Chappell, announced that they were resigning and turning the entire control back to Mr. Waltrip as the only person who possibly could pull Radio Chapel from its abyss of financial difficulties.

The Chapel founder took over at 9 o'clock Sunday morning and about 12 hours later had pledges of approximately $1,000 with which to satisfy the $2,000 judgment.

Thus, as 1938 drew to a close, Mr. Waltrip could look back upon a year during which he had dedicated his $70,000 Chapel only to come very near to losing it a few months later, during which he had won a wife and lost his assistant, ending with the problem of raising approximately $1,000 still staring him in the face.

Chapter Thirteen

CAST AWAY BECAUSE

Do not cast me away from Your presence and do not take Your Holy Spirit from me.

Psalm 51:11 (NASB)

In April 1939, with the very survival of Radio Chapel hanging in the balance, Kathryn was invited to Boston once again for the purpose of conducting her unique revival meetings. She quickly accepted the opportunity in light of the constant opposition and struggles surrounding Radio Chapel. The sustained legal assault and rumors of an impending bankruptcy in Mason City had taken a great toll on the momentum of her ministry. As a result of the judgment against Burroughs and Radio Chapel, the church's attendance and finances continued to fall. The ministry's monthly magazine, as well as the most of the daily radio broadcasts, were discontinued due to the sudden plunge in income, and all construction at the Chapel had ceased. It was one of the most difficult times in ministry Kathryn had ever faced.

The Boston trip gave Kathryn a brief but much needed reprieve from the troubles at Radio Chapel, and the evangelistic campaign would allow the preaching fire in her to burn again without the steady rain of opposition. The resistance and hostility she experienced in her "new home" of Mason City was something she hadn't encountered before. Kathryn was much more familiar with the smiling faces and welcoming hearts on display at her many revival crusades. Everywhere she went, newspapers would extol the grace and virtues of the "Girl Evangelist" in the advertisements for her upcoming meetings. In Mason City, however, Kathryn had quickly become a familiar face who was chained to a failing ministry.

The pain of persecution always stings, but perhaps never more so than when it comes from the people you love and care about. Kathryn had left her church in Denver for the people of Mason City, and she had severely reduced her traveling ministry following her marriage to Burroughs. Everything in Kathryn's life radically changed as a result of her choices and decisions. The ministry in Mason City had been effectively targeted and, as a result, had fallen on hard times. The fickle people of the region, consumed by gossip, had begun their rejection of Radio Chapel, a rejection that included Kathryn.

It had only been a month since Burroughs and Kathryn had conducted an evangelistic campaign in Nashville, Tennessee. Those meetings, which were planned to last for just two weeks, were extended to four weeks due to their success. While in Nashville, both of them preached and taught on end-time events, the Book of Revelation, and the return of Christ. Once again, the meetings were filled to capacity and the altars overflowed with people making the decision for salvation. It was in those types of meetings that Kathryn always shined and felt most free to flow with the Spirit of God.

Following their return from Nashville, Kathryn was in Mason City for just one week before departing for Boston. The campaign there was scheduled to last for two weeks, but was extended an additional week. One of the sermons preached by Kathryn, "Cast Away Because," pulled back the curtain to her wounded heart, revealing her innermost thoughts at the time regarding such topics as rejection, indifference, and sinning against the love of God.

Cast Away Because ...

Mr. Moody used to say that the Gospel is the savor of life unto life, or of death unto death, and always one or the other. He would also declare that the same sun which strikes upon the clay and hardens it would strike upon the ice and melt it, and that the hardening and softening processes were always going on in audiences where the Gospel was being preached.

It seems to me that it is almost dangerous for men to have an invitation given to them to come to God, that is, to have it given repeatedly, if it is repeatedly rejected. Some folks think they can say "yes" or "no" to God as they please. For ten years, twenty years, even thirty years, there has been a rejection of God's offer of mercy toward you.

Some of you have wandered away and some of you have lost faith in fellow Christians. Some of you have become critical of the church and even of preachers. Why? I can tell you the reason. You are in these days reaping the harvest of other days of rejection. No man may reject God continually without having his heart harden and without making it more difficult for him to turn to Jesus. I am becoming alarmed because people refuse Jesus. I have a text of Scripture that has been given to me as a warning for all such people. My text is found in the prophecy of Hosea:

My God will cast them away, because they did not hearken unto him: and they shall be wanderers among the nations.

Hosea 9:17 (KJV)

There is always a reason that God will cast people away. Then, there is another text that I think ought to be ready in connection with this which is exceedingly striking:

And ye will not come to me, that ye might have life.

John 5:40 (KJV)

My God will cast them away because ... I like to find this text of mine in the prophecy of Hosea, because Hosea himself was almost a broken-hearted man. You know the story of his wife and how she had betrayed him again and again, and yet he still loved her. He pardoned her only to be betrayed again. He took her back unto him only to have her disgrace him still again. Quivering with pain, his eyes filled with tears and with his heart almost breaking, he gives us this text. I found after studying that he gave this title to his whole prophecy: "Man's sin against love."

It is a sad thing to sin against love. Some have sinned against a mother's love. There have been those who have sinned against the love of a wife. Many have sinned against God's love. It is a sad thing that you have done it, but sadder still that you are still doing it. And, for this reason, my text is spoken: "My God will cast them away because …"

I want you to let these words sink deep into your heart. Turning over to the pages of the Old Testament, we find two or three texts that give me an illustration of man drifting from God and the very reason that Hosea said: "My God will cast them away because …"

My people are destroyed for lack of knowledge: because thou hast rejected knowledge, I will also reject thee.

Hosea 4:6 (KJV)

They refused to know. They refused to taste and see. Taken up with other things, they turned a deaf ear. So, this text reveals that one of the first steps away from God is because of preoccupation. We are too occupied with trifling things. We are too occupied with ourselves. Some are occupied in the gaining of a fortune. Others are occupied with the pursuit of pleasure. Some are occupied with sin.

Sin blinds you. It weakens you. It quiets your conscience. It takes away from you the taste for God's Word. It puts a word of criticism on your lips toward the church.

You are too occupied with other things when the greatest question in the world is:

For what shall it profit a man, if he shall gain the whole world, and lose his own soul?

Mark 8:36 (KJV)

Jesus thought your soul was important enough to say:

And if thy right eye offend thee, pluck it out, and cast it from thee: for it is profitable for thee that one of thy members should perish, and not that thy whole body should be cast into hell. And if thy right hand offend thee, cut it off, and cast it from thee: for it is profitable for thee that one of thy members should perish, and not that thy whole body should be cast into hell.

Matthew 5:29-30 (KJV)

And so Hosea says, "My God will cast them away because of the preoccupation of men." But, if this is the first step, then I think the next cause of becoming a castaway is indifference.

We have been given this true story of an old father and mother who determined to give their boy an education. They were so poor and they decided to send their boy to the university. He had to be away seven years in all. Every dollar they sent pinched the more at home. Finally, the old father said, "Wife, I cannot stand it. I'm going to see our boy." He did not have any money enough to buy a train ticket, so he hitched up his team and wagon and drove several days across the hills. The wagon in which he rode provoked a smile.

He didn't realize that his boy had drifted. He didn't know that his boy had forgotten his father's God. Three young fellows came down the street in the university town. The father saw them in the distance and his old heart began to beat rapidly as he recognized his boy. He threw down the lines and sprang out of the wagon and ran to meet his boy. The boy looked at him for a moment, and then, turning to his friends who had smiled at the old man, he told them that he did not know him. He said, "You are not my father."

The old man turned without a word. He did not touch his boy. He did not kiss him. He got into his wagon and drove back over the hills. He went back into the old farmhouse and sat down in the old chair and his head dropped forward on his breast and he was dead.

I wondered when I read the story of why the boy did not have a vision of the old days back home. I wondered why the recollection of his father's prayers did not stir him. But, I can explain that better than that of you being indifferent to Christ.

Everything that you have in life that is worth having, Christ gave to you. God gave you vision, hearing, and hands that have helped you make money. He has given to you feet that have enabled you to walk life's journey. He gave you your home, your family, and your baby.

When you have your Bible open someday, read what shall happen to those who are cast away:

Therefore thus saith the Lord GOD, Behold, my servants shall eat, but ye shall be hungry: behold, my

servants shall drink, but ye shall be thirsty: behold, my servants shall rejoice, but ye shall be ashamed.

Isaiah 65:13 (KJV)

I pity you when the crisis comes. Someday, you will reach that crisis. Death will stand outside your door and you won't be ready. You are indifferent. In God's Name, how can you be? How can you be indifferent? "My God shall cast them away because ..." And this brings me to my next passage:

Because I have called, and ye refused; I have stretched out my hand, and no man regarded;

But ye have set at nought all my counsel, and would none of my reproof:

I also will laugh at your calamity; I will mock when your fear cometh;

When your fear cometh as desolation, and your destruction cometh as a whirlwind; when distress and anguish cometh upon you.

Then shall they call upon me, but I will not answer; they shall seek me early, but they shall not find me:

For that they hated knowledge, and did not choose the fear of the LORD:

Proverbs 1:24-29 (KJV)

Yes, this third and awful step is the step of willful rejection. Willful rejection makes you like the man who ran away from a police officer in New York and ran down to the river and jumped off the dock into the water. The policeman threw a rope to him and it was too short. He threw another and it landed across his arm and he came up and grabbed it, and began to twine around his arm. Then, with an oath, he cast the rope away saying, "To hell with your rope," and then sank out of sight.

You have done the same thing with God. He called you when you were a boy. He called you when the marriage bells were pealing. He called you when your first baby came and went into the grave. He called you when your mother passed away. And you have been as the one thief who hung by the side of Christ and willfully rejected His love and mercy and grace.

"My God will cast them away because …" The last text and the last cause of being cast away has to do with blasphemy:

But they refused to hearken, and pulled away the shoulder, and stopped their ears, that they should not hear. Yea, they made their hearts as an adamant stone, lest they should hear the law, and the words which the LORD of hosts hath sent in his spirit by the former prophets: therefore came a great wrath from the LORD of hosts. Therefore it is come to pass, that as he cried, and they would not hear; so they cried, and I would not hear, saith the LORD of hosts: But I scattered them with a whirlwind among all the nations whom they knew not. Thus the land was desolate after them, that no man passed through nor returned: for they laid the pleasant land desolate.

Zechariah 7:11–14 (KJV)

Listen, how many times have you rejected God? Stop and think. I do not ask you how many times you have rejected your pastor. If it is only a man's appeal, then drive it out of your mind with a song. Go on and eat, drink, and be merry. But, if it is God's call, how in God's Name can you reject Him?

I believe the greatest sin today is the sin against love. When a mother bends over her sick child, the more she loves her child, the more she suffers. If the child dies, the pain is indescribable. But, if the child sins and the boy she used to hold on her knees, whose lips she used to kiss, into whose eyes she used to look, if that boy came staggering home drunk, can any word describe her pain?

God is like that. You thought you could dismiss or forget Him, but He still loves you. But listen, that love can be broken. God will not always seek you out. There's coming a day when His Spirit will not always strive with man.

"My God will cast them away because ..." Can you tell me what is the greatest sin in the world? A poor girl who was deceived in her childhood and lost that which made her life sweet and beautiful says, "Sir, I know what the greatest sin is." No, child, it is not that.

A mother, with care written in every expression of her countenance, her hair gray and her back bent at only 50 years of age is a drunkard's wife, and she says, "I have waited for him and he never came. I have gone hungry that my babes might have a crust of bread. I know what is the greatest sin." But, I answered, "No, dear woman, you do not know. It is not that."

There is a young man who is being eaten away by a horrible disease and he has lost the light of his eye and he knows there is nothing for him but shame and disgrace. He says, "I know what is the greatest sin." I respond, "No, fellow, you do not know. It is not that."

The greatest sin in the world is the rejection of Jesus Christ. "My God will cast them away because ..."

But, I would not leave you with this. Oh, if God would only give me some new way to plead. If only He would give me some new means by which I could appeal to you now and bend the will that has been as hard as iron and touch the heart that has been as flinty as rock.

Turn ye, oh, turn ye, for why will ye die? Today, if you will hear His voice, harden not your hearts. Seek the Lord while He may be found. Call upon Him while He is near. May God help us seek Him tonight.

Chapter Fourteen

ONLY A MIRACLE CAN SAVE RADIO CHAPEL

And the rain descended, and the floods came, and the winds blew, and beat upon that house; and it fell: and great was the fall of it.

Matthew 7:27 (KJV)

Just a year prior, the future of Radio Chapel seemed very bright with plans being made for its dedication celebration and parade. Only twenty-three short months had passed since the vision for ministry was put before the people in an old weathered revival tent, a vision that culminated with the construction of the magnificent dream church. Now, as a result of relentless attacks and persecution from within and from without, the dream was hanging on by a thread—a thread that was about to break.

The days of difficulty had turned into weeks, and the weeks into months. The long, hard grind of opposition had taken a bitter toll upon Radio Chapel, leaving it in an unsustainable and financially vulnerable position. There was no denying it—collapse was imminent. The vultures were circling closer than ever before as the adversaries of the ministry grew day by day. Radio Chapel, stressed to its breaking point by financial attacks, religious resistance, and internal division, now found itself entering a season of abandonment. Nobody wants to go down with the ship, much less contribute his or her money toward the seemingly lost cause of repairing the damage needed to keep it afloat.

The shifting sands upon which Radio Chapel was built were diverse, but perhaps the most lethal proved to be the failure to simply count the cost. The cost of rapid success. The cost of massive indebtedness. The cost of celebrity ministry turned to familiarity. The cost of envy and jealousy. The cost of gossip and betrayal. The cost of attempting something that had never been done. These realities, coupled with the enormous headwinds of legal losses and mounting liens, proved to be intolerable. On Monday, May 15, 1939, the *Globe Gazette* broke the sad story that so many Radio Chapel supporters hoped would never come.

Only a Miracle Can Save Radio Chapel

The future of the two-year career of Burroughs A. Waltrip's Radio Chapel was in doubt Monday with an announcement by the director that a petition for receivership is to be filed in district court.

With tears in his eyes and voice, Mr. Waltrip Sunday night told his audience in the $70,000 modernistic Chapel building that only a miracle within the next day or two could save the doors from closing.

"A loan of $25,000 with which to pay off outstanding debts was the only thing which could prevent the filing of the receivership," he said. He asked the audience to give him $100 in order to pay his personal bills and start anew in some other town. The collection totaled approximately $35.

When questioned after the service, the Louisiana Pul-piteer said that he did not have any plans to move out of Mason City for the present and that he and Mrs. Waltrip would stay here until the final outcome was established.

Concerning the future of the Chapel, he said that he hoped the receivers would see fit to hire him to carry on the work. During the service, he revealed that during the brighter days of Radio Chapel, the weekly income totaled $250, but that during the last several weeks the income was not sufficient to meet operating expenses.

He warned businessmen against purchasing the Radio Chapel property to establish a business enterprise on the location.

"No business will ever prosper here," he asserted, warning businessmen to "keep their hands off the house of God," and calling attention to the failure of a business to prosper in another building in Mason City which formerly had been used as a church.

As he warmed to his theme, he shouted dramatically that there is a curse on Mason City. "The people of this town have turned down the house of God and I feel sorry for Mason City because of it."

A meeting of the Chapel congregation will be conducted in the Hotel Hanford Tuesday evening at 7:45 o'clock by himself and Mrs. Waltrip, the director announced.

Highlights of Radio Chapel's career in Mason City were reviewed by Mr. Waltrip during his service. He pointed out that the Chapel started in a tent on July 17, 1937, and progressed to the present $70,000 building.

The downfall of the Chapel organization repeatedly was blamed by the pulpiteer on the rift between himself and the board of directors. He explained that the trouble culminated in December over financial matters, and he resigned only to resume control four days later.

The Andrew Kaduce trial was another factor in the downhill slide of the Chapel, Mr. Waltrip explained, and cost the organization $2,100 which was collected by freewill offerings. He stated that the trial occurred when Andrew Kaduce was declared of unsound mind and his brother George Kaduce got a judgment against Radio Chapel for the $2,100 donation previously given by Andrew.

As Mr. Waltrip dramatically outlined the career of the Chapel, sobs were audible in the congregation, and each time he railed against "those who have double-crossed me," applause burst out from the audience.

Following their parting of ways, Keith and Burroughs found themselves overseeing divided congregations. Keith and Mary began conducting independent revival meetings at the local YMCA in a futile attempt to minister to the ever-growing group of disenchanted and confused believers. Burroughs and Kathryn endeavored to stabilize the Radio Chapel ministry while staving off the efforts of creditors as public opinion worsened. Gone were the days of lighthearted fellowship over breakfast and thoughtful collaboration on sermons. The sweeter times of laughter and planning for the future were set aside for the miserable task of damage control. Like a tidal wave swamping a house and then retreating, great destruction had been done in a brief moment of time, leaving behind the dreadful scene of a ministry that was spinning out of control.

Almost daily, the regional newspapers published the despairing news of the Chapel's demise. The rash of articles dissected the details of Radio Chapel's financial woes, setbacks, and internal struggles. On May 16, 1939, the *Globe Gazette* reported that a temporary receiver for Radio Chapel had been appointed upon the voluntary application of Burroughs. The court then set May 29 as the time for a hearing on the application to make the appointment of the receiver permanent. Attached to the petition was a list of debts totaling $45,260.16, the result of 34 liens that had been filed against the Chapel. According to courthouse records, the largest lien was in the amount of $12,194.62 and the smallest was only $2.56. A number of former Chapel members and directors also took the opportunity to file claims against the ministry, including Verne Mettler who was invited to speak during dedication week and subsequently filed a claim to collect $100 that he had donated for the Chapel construction. According to the newspaper, the petition was filed by Burroughs in order to protect the interests of his creditors. Unfortunately, Burroughs and Kathryn were unable to fend off the onslaught of financial troubles and steer their ministry clear of bankruptcy. They had run out of time, extensions, and money. Like a damaged ship having taken on too much water, Radio Chapel's descent was fast approaching. The article read in part:

Goodbye. God Bless You Good Everybody.

Radio Chapel Tuesday morning concluded its 18-month series of broadcasts over KGLO without any mention of the pending difficulty. Mr. Waltrip merely finished his last broadcast with his usual, "Goodbye, God bless you good everybody." The radio station announcer made the statement that it was the final broadcast.

The Louisiana Pulpiteer centered his entire broadcast on an inspirational sermon dealing strictly with religious subjects. During previous financial crises at Radio Chapel, Mr. Waltrip has frequently utilized his morning broadcasts for money requests.

Radio Chapel started in a tent on July 17, 1937, and under the direction of Mr. Waltrip has progressed to a modernistic $70,000 building complete with a disappearing pulpit, indirect lighting, opera seats and an array of blinking stars in the stage background.

The first public announcement of the receivership decision came Sunday night as Mr. Waltrip, with tears in his eyes, stood in the Chapel pulpit and stated that "only a miracle within the next day or two can save the Chapel doors from closing."

Like quicksand, everything finally closed in on Radio Chapel during that final week. With church attendance hovering around one hundred people, ten percent of what it was at its height, Kathryn was seen weeping openly during those final services. The months of agony and spiritual frustration were no longer held back as Burroughs and Kathryn accepted the inevitable fate of their ministry in Mason City. The last message listed on the *Globe Gazette's* religion page preached by Burroughs in May 1939 was, "I Know He Lives." Likewise, the last message preached by Kathryn was, "In God's School." On Tuesday, May 16, the local sheriff walked up to Radio Chapel and nailed the notice of receivership to the front doors. Accompanying the sheriff was a locksmith who changed the locks on the Chapel doors.

"We hadn't seen much of them during their last months in Mason City," said Keith as his fingers lightly brushed the old photographs of Burroughs and Kathryn that lay before him. "It wasn't Burroughs' or Kathryn's fault. We served with them. People got the story all wrong. Burroughs was right when he identified the spirit of suspicion." After pausing, Keith continued, "That spirit of suspicion closed the church. We don't know why they left so quickly. We loved them."

Mary, dabbing tears from her eyes, whispered, "We had good times together. We had wonderful times together, because we were thick with them."

Late Tuesday evening, with both Burroughs' and Kathryn's cars packed for their departure, Burroughs picked up the telephone and made one final call to Keith and Mary Williams. The friends and ministry companions were about to reunite one last time. Keith and Mary drove the short distance to the Hotel Hanford, dreading the imminent farewells. "They were very sad," Keith mentioned. "So very, very sad." Mary added, "It was such a shame it was destroyed. We never saw them again after that night."

The front page of the newspaper on Wednesday, May 17, 1939, read, "Waltrip Says Farewell to Mason City—Evangelist Accompanied to City Limits by Horn Tooting Parade."

> Burroughs A. Waltrip, director of the bankrupt Radio Chapel, left Mason City Tuesday night accompanied to the city limits by two dozen carloads of followers in a horn-tooting impromptu farewell parade.
>
> "I may not leave Mason City with bands playing and flags waving as I have often stated I would," said the evangelist as he suggested the parade to the congregation, "but I hope you will make as big a showing as possible."
>
> Mr. Waltrip made the announcement of his leaving at the final meeting of the Chapel congregation in the Hotel Hanford Tuesday evening. He explained that he would conduct an evangelistic tour through the southern states and visit Mason City in a few weeks.
>
> As the Louisiana Pulpiteer drove away in a 1939 Buick, accompanied by the horn-tooting followers, approximately 50 members of the congregation lined North Federal

Avenue, waving handkerchiefs, and shouting, "God Bless You!"

Mrs. Waltrip left for Des Moines in her car earlier in the day where the couple is scheduled to start the tour. Mr. Waltrip explained to the congregation Tuesday evening that his wife could not attend because it was too much of a strain on her nerves.

After the announcement that he was leaving, the approximately 125 members attending the meeting gave the pulpiteer about $114 as a gift. Previously during the meeting he stated, "I am not taking with me a single dollar that was raised in Radio Chapel."

Mr. Waltrip explained emphatically during the meeting that he had no word of criticism for the creditors of Radio Chapel and he heartily endorsed the temporary receiver for the Chapel.

Mr. Waltrip termed watching the receivership sign being tacked on the Chapel doors as, "a major operation without an anesthetic." Later he expressed his belief that in a few weeks he would have the privilege of pulling out the tacks and burning the sign.

"As a city project, Radio Chapel would do Mason City more good than a million dollar industry," the director pointed out as he expressed his disappointment that the city did not support his project.

In the weeks following Radio Chapel's bankruptcy and Burroughs' and Kathryn's exit from Mason City, the courts conveniently ruled that Andrew Kaduce was, "no longer a person of unsound mind," and was, "no longer a proper subject of guardianship." On September 11, 1939, a few months after the Chapel was forced into receivership, the judge declared Andrew to be of a sound mind and that he was no longer a spendthrift influenced by religious fervor. With the filing of the court's final reports, Andrew's business assets and property were returned to him. After legal fees were dispersed to their respective attorneys, approximately $300 remained of the original $2,100 lawsuit. Interestingly, the lead attorney that headed up the lawsuit against Burroughs and Radio Chapel died suddenly in his home three months later in Mason City on Christmas Day, 1939, at the age of 36. The Radio Chapel facility, which stood empty for over six months, was quietly sold to a local Baptist minister, who in turn sold it to KGLO Radio. KGLO Radio was the very same station from which Burroughs and Kathryn previously broadcast their messages.

Salt in the Wound

As a final insult to the Radio Chapel takedown, the Mason City Chamber of Commerce, during their annual Christmas Party, set their sights on the bankrupted ministry. The newspaper reported, "1,000 Roar at Chamber of Commerce Christmas Party," as a record crowd turned out for an evening that parodied and paraded the events of the year before an all-time high attendance which included community leaders, bankers, and various ministers. Advertised as, "The People and Events of 1939: Butt of Fun," the singers, dressed as hillbillies, took the stage in the lobby of the Hotel Hanford, which was the former home of Burroughs and Kathryn, singing and playing several numbers. The Radio Chapel skit was the main event, and included a number of performers flinging quips back and forth amongst themselves.

Part of the minstrel gags, according to the Mason City *Globe Gazette*, included the hillbilly singers interrupting one another with choruses about the downfall and subsequent large amount of money made by others off of Radio Chapel's demise. The first singer began with the chorus:

> *Radio Chapel with Waltrip away,*
>
> *That's where I took a task,*
>
> *Oh, what a task that's come to stay.*
>
> *And now as I ponder,*
>
> *My thoughts ever stray,*
>
> *To Radio Chapel with Waltrip away.*

Just then, the singer was interrupted in mid-song when the master of ceremonies handed a scripted note to him that called him a "smart guy" and told him to get up to date on the Radio Chapel. This he proceeded to do with the new words:

> *Radio Chapel with Waltrip away*
>
> *That was my task, you call it task,*
>
> *I found it play.*
>
> *And now as I wonder,*
>
> *My thoughts ever stray,*
>
> *To Radio Chapel and what it will pay.*

They thought it a problem,

A tough one to face,

Just for a little while,

Then they found I had sold the place.

I'm happy to say,

Of Radio Chapel,

With Waltrip away.

Oh, I sighed when I took on the Chapel,

Never dreaming how lucky I'd be,

And I cried as I thought of the Chapel,

And what there'd be in it for me.

Radio Chapel 'twas my lucky day,

When I discovered fifty thousand bucks,

I will ever pray,

For Radio Chapel with Waltrip away.

Toward the end of the evening's frivolities, the Hotel Hanford's general manager conducted a drawing for the "canned ham" award to be presented to the "ham" or rather, the "pig," of the city. The first staged name drawn was that of the Reverend Burroughs Waltrip, which the announcer spoke slowly with haughty disdain. The people laughed as it was shared he was not in attendance for obvious reasons. Ralph Geer, who had served as Burroughs' and Kathryn's pianist while they were at Radio Chapel, supplied the music for the Chamber of Commerce event, which was particularly repugnant being that just months earlier, he had served at their side in ministry. A photograph of Ralph laughing at the mockery of Radio Chapel was included at the top of the newspaper article.

Like the Apostle Paul, Burroughs and Kathryn discovered what it was like to be stoned by the very same people who had just months earlier celebrated them. The two of them learned all too well a lesson that the people who were once for you can quickly turn against you, and the word for that action is betrayal.

"We need have no fear so long as we keep faith in God. Sin is our greatest enemy. We also must have the spiritual power of the people," Burroughs once sadly said. "That will give the final answer of victory or defeat."

Chapter Fifteen

FULL CIRCLE

**From the beginning I revealed the end. From long ago
I told you things that had not yet happened, saying, "My
plan will stand, and I'll do everything I intended to do."**

Isaiah 46:10 (God's Word)

In early September 2007, I once again received a telephone call
from Gladys who served as Keith and Mary's personal assistant,
in Watertown, South Dakota. She was contacting me to let me
know that Keith and Mary had their hearts set on visiting Mason
City, where their ministry began, one last time. Both of them were
dealing with health issues which, combined with their advanced age,
would eventually make the five hour drive impossible should they
delay it any longer. Keith and Mary were both 92 years old. Keith
wanted to speak with me, but it was difficult for him to hear me
over the phone, so Gladys spoke on his behalf. She asked if the
upcoming trip would be a good time for us to meet once again and

fellowship. I told Gladys it would be our distinct honor to accommodate Keith and Mary and that I would count it a privilege to host them for their visit. I asked her for the date of their upcoming trip and she told me they would arrive in Mason City on Saturday, September 8, 2007, and depart on Sunday. Since the Williams' plans involved being in town over the weekend, I extended an invitation for them to come be a part of our Sunday morning service. Gladys said they would be thrilled to join us.

Having spoken so much of Keith and Mary and the fascinating account of Radio Chapel to my congregation, they now felt like family to our church. I genuinely cherished our times together and many hours visiting with them in Watertown, as well as our conversations over the telephone. It didn't seem possible that I had only known them for less than two years. It felt like I had known them a lifetime. They were especially like family to me now, and I knew the feeling was mutual.

Keith and Mary had entrusted me with so much precious history in such a short amount of time. Scrapbooks and mailers. Sermon outlines and articles. Old photographs and newspaper clippings. Interviews and narratives surrounding the Radio Chapel timeline. Then beyond that, there was so much more. They opened their lives to me, taking me by the heart and leading me into the short life of Radio Chapel. They invited me to experience all of Radio Chapel's successes and failures, mountaintops and valleys, and its aspirations and heartbreaks. The living history that they so selflessly offered up transported me back into the days of Burroughs and Kathryn and acquainted me with a tale that continued to overwhelm me. I felt like I had been introduced to the Kathryn they knew so long ago. The journey through time that I travelled with them was unforgettable. However, it was not yet complete.

In anticipation of their upcoming visit, I began to make plans to share the details with my congregation at our mid-week service. There was an abundance of Radio Chapel information that I was still processing, so I decided it would be best for me to assemble some type of historical narrative to bring before my people. I had been diligently compiling a thorough timeline of the Radio Chapel era along with how those years both related to and affected Kathryn Kuhlman's ministry. While preparing my notes from the numerous copies of faded newspaper articles, one title in particular from the Radio Chapel era immediately caught my attention: "Revival Tent On Chapel Site: First Spade Of Dirt For Foundation To Be Turned Tuesday." The date at the top of the Mason City *Globe Gazette* newspaper was September 13, 1937.

Could it be that Keith and Mary were set to travel back to Mason City the very week that construction on Radio Chapel began exactly seventy years ago? I took a deep breath and sat back in my chair as I attempted to comprehend and process what was unfolding before my eyes. My mind quickly raced back to the prophecy from our church service in November 2005:

"I will set right that which is wrong and I will do that which has not been done, and together we will finish that which was begun. That which was begun years ago shall see its day and shall see its hour. It shall spring forth. Justice is Mine, and I will redeem from the hands of the enemy that which has been lost for decades, and I will bring it back in the **_seventieth_** year. As it was in the days of Daniel, so shall it be in your day. I will resurrect that which has been trodden in the mud. No man shall withstand it. No one shall hold it back. For this is My time, and this is My Church, and this is My way. It shall happen on My appointed season. It shall spring forth. It shall spring from Heaven, and it shall do what I have called it to do."

Suddenly, the Williams' upcoming visit took on new meaning. There was much more transpiring than the human eye could see. The Lord had been working unnoticed behind the scene all the while, but now the invisible was slowly becoming visible. There is no coincidence in God. There is neither chance nor happenstance in Him. He is always advancing His plan while causing all things to "work together." His providence is powerful, like a river, and it guides our life's ship through the passage of time. We are but the willing vessels in this river. Even though the plan of God takes time, we must wait patiently for it. The Bible tells us in Habakkuk that the vision operates in a certain way:

> **Then the LORD answered me and said,**
> **"Record the vision**
> **And inscribe it on tablets,**
> **That the one who reads it may run.**
> **For the vision is yet for the appointed time;**
> **It hastens toward the goal and it will not fail.**
> **Though it tarries, wait for it;**
> **For it will certainly come, it will not delay."**
>
> **Habakkuk 2:2-3 (NASB)**

THE APPOINTED TIME

It was now the appointed time. We had waited for it and the time had come. The vision of God would not fail. The morning of Sunday, September 9, was unlike any other. The word had spread of Keith and Mary's visit, and the story was even covered by the local newspaper and the television station. As a result of my sharing the Radio Chapel story, the congregation was charged with anticipation. We all knew it was going to be a special day and one to remember. The excitement in the atmosphere was only exceeded by the excitement in my own heart. I knew that I was in the center of God's will and that it was time to experience great and mighty things. The words of Jeremiah the Prophet echoed throughout my spirit all morning before the service:

Call unto me, and I will answer thee, and shew thee great and mighty things, which thou knowest not.

Jeremiah 33:3 (KJV)

I had the great honor of introducing the associate pastors of Radio Chapel that morning. As our ushers assisted Keith and Mary to the platform, the congregation gave them a five-minute standing ovation. That dear couple stood there and wept as a flood of emotion overwhelmed them. As my wife and I took the stage, we embraced them as the people continued to clap and cheer. Throughout my entire life I have heard the words, "God's timing is always perfect. He is never early and He is never late. He is always right on time." I had preached that principle myself and had heard it preached many times as well. But now standing there, I really understood it. As the people were being seated, I began to share the history of my journey, beginning with the prophecy from November 2005, and continuing up to present day. Keith stood next to me and Mary, who was weeping, stood next to Lisa.

For the next fifteen minutes, Keith and Mary poured out their hearts as they shared about the pioneering of Radio Chapel and their call to ministry. Keith, the aged preacher, held the microphone in his shaky hand as he shared about how it all began:

"We attended the service with Burroughs and Kathryn on a Sunday afternoon. The next day, Monday morning, I received a phone call from Burroughs and he said, 'Will you come to the Hanford Hotel? I want to talk to you about something.' So, I said, 'Yes, I'll come.'

"I went over to the Hanford Hotel and went up the elevator and went to his room and knocked on the door. When Burroughs opened the door, he fell on his knees and prayed. When he got up, he said, 'I'm looking for help and I need your help. I want you to become our associate pastor and associate worker. We're going to build a Chapel here.' I said, 'Are you sure?' and they said, 'Yes, we're sure.' That was the beginning. Then I said, 'When should I begin?' They responded by saying I could start whenever I could get away from the Firestone company, and I said, 'That will be the next day then.' Then we hugged each other. I was happy for them and they were happy for me. Those were exciting days when we were there. We were right there with them all of the time. It was a privilege to serve with them."

Then, as Mary was handed the microphone, she began to pray. "Father, it's a hundred times over worth it to obey You, and we are so amazed at how You work and what You bring before us, Lord. We want to be more faithful and serve You to the best of our ability so that people will come to know You in a personal way. We thank You that You have done it all and we've been willing to follow You."

Keith then closed the prayer, "Father, this brings back memories of Radio Chapel, and we are here giving You the glory for the victory. We have to serve together, and then build together, in order to win together. Even though doors were closed, many other doors have been opened, and we thank You that the plan of God is always continuing."

It was a magnificent moment as everything came full circle that morning. "Full Circle" was the name of my message at that service. It was surreal as Keith and Mary sat in the front row of our church, exactly seventy years later, listening to a message about their lives and ministry. I preached about the restoring hand of God as I ministered from my text found in Jeremiah:

> **For thus says the LORD, "When seventy years have been completed for Babylon, I will visit you and fulfill My good word to you, to bring you back to this place. For I know the plans that I have for you," declares the LORD, "plans for welfare and not for calamity to give you a future and a hope. Then you will call upon Me and come and**

pray to Me, and I will listen to you. You will seek Me and find Me when you search for Me with all your heart."
Jeremiah 29:10-13 (NASB)

Returning to my office following the service, we sat together with Keith and Mary and fellowshipped like old friends. Both of them were visibly moved with both happiness and tears by the day's events. We shared, laughed, and prayed for one another. We also gave God thanks for our friendship and for what He had done between us.

As our time together that morning drew to a close, Keith motioned for me to come over to where he was seated. As I approached him, he motioned for me to lean down even closer so that he could speak to me. As I knelt on one knee, he placed his hand on my shoulder and began to weep as he charged me.

"Shane," he said, "thank you for what you have done. Keep on preaching for the Lord. It's wonderful to see the spirit of Radio Chapel continued like this. Thank you for your friendship and for being a part of our lives and ministry. It's up to you to carry on now." For as long as I live, I will never forget the day Keith Williams laid his hands upon me—the man who had Kathryn Kuhlman's hands laid upon him—and commissioned me with continuing their ministry.

An especially poignant moment took place just before Keith and Mary departed from Mason City that day. Keith asked if we could possibly stop at the Radio Chapel building, which still stands today, so that he could see it one final time. We drove them to the building located in downtown Mason City, and, as we walked up to the front doors, Keith stepped off the sidewalk and walked over to behind the bushes to the right of the entrance doors. Pushing aside the shrubs, he revealed the cornerstone with the name "Burroughs A. Waltrip" inscribed into the stone. Under Burroughs name was written, "Radio Chapel—A.D. 1938." Keith slowly ran his hand over Burroughs' name, pausing to say, "I was right here when they put this cornerstone in place," as he pointed to the ground beneath his feet. "Burroughs was there," he said, pointing to another place a few feet away, "Kathryn was there, and Mary stood there."

Keith still referred to it as "his" Radio Chapel. He took the time to point out where the various offices were back in the days of the Chapel, and where each of them worked while serving in ministry there. Stepping back onto the sidewalk, the four of us posed for pictures in front of the building. Keith knew this was the last time he would ever see Radio Chapel again and it was evident he desired to linger as long as possible. As we prepared to leave, Keith walked up to the doors and pulled on the handles one final time. It was heart-wrenching as he turned to say, "The doors are still locked."

THE FINISHED COURSE

On July 3, 2009, Keith laid down his earthly body and stepped over into glory at the age of 94. Precious in the eyes of the Lord is the death of His saints. Having faithfully preached the Gospel of Jesus Christ and diligently executed the charge given to him by Kathryn Kuhlman for seventy years, our church was the last church Keith ever spoke in. When Gladys contacted me to tell me of his death, she informed me one of Keith's last requests on his deathbed was: "I would like Reverend Philpott to bring the message for my funeral. I would really appreciate that." According to Gladys, his very last words were, "Be sure to greet everyone for me."

As we traveled to Watertown on Tuesday, July 7, I was humbled by the immensity of recent events and the unfolding revelation of Kathryn's season at Radio Chapel. How does one tell this story? How is anyone able to capture and convey the depth and meaning of those events? How does one bring honor to an event in time that has been so dishonored and misunderstood? It is nearly impossible to do without the assistance of God. His timing and accuracy are so amazing that it is almost impossible to describe with human words.

Radio Chapel had so impacted Reverend Keith Williams that he constructed a chapel on his own ministry grounds decades later that was an almost exact replica of the Mason City Radio Chapel. It was like traveling through time as we approached Keith's chapel for his funeral. The size and shape of the building was the same as Radio Chapel. The interior layout was the same, right down to the platform and pulpit. What an enduring mark Radio Chapel had made upon his life.

We held his "celebration of life" service in that building as his close friends and ministry partners from around the nation and the world gathered to honor his legacy of faith. With great humility, I spoke of Keith's call from God and the ministry of his life. I related the story of Kathryn ordaining him and laying her hands upon him and delivering to him the charge for ministry. We laughed and cried together as the accounts of God's faithfulness found their new home in the hearts of the hearers. I shared with those present about God's divine appointments, how Keith and I met, and our journey of discovery with one another. Now, precisely seventy years after Burroughs and Kathryn departed from Radio Chapel after entrusting their sermons to him in 1939, Keith departed from this world after entrusting those same sermons to me. Like seeds on the wind, the Radio Chapel story went forth once more in the hearts and minds of those guests and ministers present on that day.

Burroughs and Kathryn always focused on one primary thing in their respective ministries: The salvation of souls. Their passion and vision lived on through Keith's ministry and was evident in a song that he had written which he titled, "The Bells of Heaven." Keith wrote the song in 1992 while staying at a Chinese missionary house in Davao City in the Philippines, and it was reprinted in the funeral bulletin at his request:

The Bells of Heaven

The bells of Heaven ring out ev'ry day
For the souls who've been won who once were astray,
But our task is not done for there is still much to do
For many are the tribes that are waiting for you.

Others who feel like the rich man of old
Go down to the depths for they're not in the fold.
Dear friend of the Gospel, let us not fail them now,
But give and keep giving as our means will allow.

The bells will ring out as we show them the way,

And the angels will sing for the souls who did pray.

Let's be true to our task Jesus gave us to do,

And we, like the Angels, will rejoice too.

Chorus:

So let us pray ev'ry day, and give as you can

That God's Word may be found and given to man.

They are reaching each day for the crumbs from your table

Like Lazarus of old, Let us give while we're able

("The Bells of Heaven" by Keith Williams, 1992.)

Mary passed away and went on to her Heavenly reward on Saturday, July 10, 2010, at the age of 95. I believe with all of my heart, they heard the words, "Well done, good and faithful servants. You have been faithful over a few things, now I will make you ruler over much. Come and enter into the joy of your Lord."

LIFE LESSONS

It would seem that God's plan always involves flawed men and women. It is in the weaknesses of mankind that He is seen as being strong. Keith always felt that Burroughs and Kathryn were judged too harshly by people who chose to dwell on the negative rather than give them credit for all the good they did. He especially admired Kathryn for what she had accomplished in ministry, wherever her life's journey took her. "How much of a price does a person have to pay for one failure," Keith once asked me. "Kathryn believed in forgiveness and she believed the Lord forgave, and she went on."

In the mad rush to assign blame and demonize Burroughs and Kathryn, most people ignore the most important thing: The truth. The truth is that Radio Chapel wasn't brought down by their relationship, by prior mistakes or missteps, but rather it was struck down by the same age-old demons and strongholds that great men and women and churches have faced for centuries. Jealously. Strife. False brethren. Legal opposition. Governmental intrusion. Persecution. These things, when coupled with the Satanic forces which are unleashed by gossip and suspicion, always lead to rebellion and betrayal. However, the truth stands for anyone willing to look for it.

Burroughs Waltrip, Kathryn Kuhlman, and Keith and Mary Williams were part of something bigger than life itself. Tragically, Burroughs was never seen nor heard from again after his divorce from Kathryn in April 1947. To this present day, no one knows what became of him, not even his sons or his extended family. Most disturbingly, Burroughs never did again see his sons from his previous marriage following his divorce from Jessie. No one knows how he lived or how he died, or where he is even buried.

Kathryn, on the other hand, proved that the gates of Hell cannot prevail against the Church. When a caterpillar enters its cocoon, one of two things will happen. It will either transform into a butterfly, or it will die. No matter which scenario takes place, it will never leave that cocoon again as a caterpillar. So it was with Kathryn Kuhlman. Kathryn demonstrated through her unyielding faith in God that when the worst thing that can happen does in fact happen, the future is still bright. And like a butterfly, she also demonstrated the strength to fly on the wind can only come after exerting the strength necessary to crawl out of the dirt.

The life lessons of Kathryn and her season at Radio Chapel are many, but some ring louder than others for us today. God always has a plan, and the plan of God always goes on. His plan is a mighty moving force that cannot be stopped, and it will yield for neither man nor Satan.

Defeat can be overcome and what has been lost can be regained, and while adversity and opposition might delay our victory, they will not win in the end. Through faith and diligence, against all odds, it will be the servant of God who wins in the end. This is the promise and reward given in God's Word to believers for their unwavering perseverance.

Look to yourselves (take care) that you may not lose (throw away or destroy) all that we and you have labored for, but that you may [persevere until you] win and receive back a perfect reward [in full].

2 John 8 (AMP)

In the telling of this story, these timeless sermons and messages now breathe new life once again. Whenever this account is read or shared, Kathryn's sermons are preached again. Every time someone's heart is stirred or a life is impacted or changed, she speaks again. In reality, Kathryn Kuhlman's evangelistic crusades never ended, they simply continue on in a much different way. Even though the speaker may die, their words never quit speaking.

God's prophetic words to me proved true. He has set right that which was wrong, and together we have finished what was begun. The will of God sprang forth and He redeemed from the enemy what was lost for decades. And He did it in the seventieth year as He promised. God has resurrected that which was trodden in the mud, and in His appointed season, it is doing what He has called it to do. The true account of Kathryn Kuhlman and Radio Chapel can now be known for all those who are lovers of the truth. Were it not for the hand of God and the divine appointments which He set in place, the true story of Kathryn's Radio Chapel years may have very well been lost to history and her messages of faith and victory not been discovered.

Tuesday, May 16, 1939, was the last time Keith and Mary saw Burroughs and Kathryn on this earth. Following their last hug, as Keith stood in the doorway with their sermons clutched in his hands, the sad goodbyes were spoken. The parting words of wisdom which Kathryn spoke to Keith and Mary at that final farewell echo down to us through the years. As Kathryn consoled her young friends, gently wiping the tears from their faces, she softly said,

"Always remember,

obey the reading of the Word,

obey the leading of the Spirit,

and keep going until Jesus says, 'No more.'"

CONCLUSION

After a long time the lord of those servants cometh, and reckoneth with them. And so he that had received five talents came and brought other five talents, saying, Lord, thou deliveredst unto me five talents: behold, I have gained beside them five talents more. His lord said unto him, Well done, thou good and faithful servant: thou hast been faithful over a few things, I will make thee ruler over many things: enter thou into the joy of thy lord.

Matthew 25:19-21 (KJV)

It has always been the nature of hateful people to attempt to crush the gifts and callings that God has entrusted to His servants, and it will continue to be so until Christ's return. The Apostle Paul wrote, *"Finally, brethren, pray for us that the word of the Lord will spread rapidly and be glorified, just as it did also with you; and that we will be rescued from perverse and evil men; for not all have faith"* (2 Thessalonians 3:1-2, NASB). One of Satan's most effective methods for hindering the spread of the Gospel is to use faithless people to attack and slander the efforts of God's preachers. Burroughs Waltrip, Kathryn Kuhlman, and the Radio Chapel in Mason City, Iowa, encountered overwhelming opposition both inside and outside the walls of their own church and the opposition was successful in thwarting the spread of the Gospel in that area for quite some time. As a preacher, it must have been a horrible thing for

Kathryn to behold false brethren – perverse and evil people – side with the enemy in order to reject and betray her. Had she succumbed to that assault and buried her talents in shame, the world would have never been exposed to her great faith and passion for Jesus Christ. However, like the proverbial Phoenix that rose from the ashes, Kathryn did just the same by overcoming the adversity and dishonor that visited her life. She discovered that rejection and betrayal in one city did not equate to rejection and betrayal in the rest of the nation.

Entrusting herself to the limitless grace and mercy of the Heavenly Father, Kathryn pulled herself back from the brink of ministerial ruin and redoubled her efforts for the Kingdom of God. She would never be content with burying her talents; she refused to live her life without ever having seen what God could do through her. Paul went on to say, *"But the Lord is faithful, and He will strengthen and protect you from the evil one"* (2 Thessalonians 3:3, NASB). Kathryn placed her faith in the strength and faithfulness of God, reengaged, and never looked back. The rest, as they say, is history.

Following Kathryn's experience at Radio Chapel, she traveled extensively throughout the United States and many other countries conducting healing and miracle crusades. At these popular crusades, thousands of people came to receive Jesus Christ as their Savior. Kathryn's unique preaching style, coupled with her personal transparency, broke through all denominational barriers, paving the path for a ministry that became known for the miraculous. Despite the abuse experienced in her ministry's early years, Kathryn never lost her humility, her tenderness or her compassion. She learned firsthand that God causes all things to work together for good to those who love Him, to those who are called according to His purpose (Romans 8:28). In time, Kathryn became one of the most recognized and admired ministers in the world.

It would be difficult to accurately gauge the positive impact of Kathryn Kuhlman's ministry upon the faith movement of the Twentieth Century. The awareness that she brought to the Person of the Holy Spirit clearly set her apart from many preachers of her time. Kathryn influenced numerous ministers of the Gospel through her passionate, yet simple trust in the power of the Holy Spirit. Throughout the years, the fruit of Kathryn Kuhlman's ministry has stood the test of time and many today regard her as an authentic and important forerunner to the Word of Faith movement.

History is now witness to the fact that the vision and innovation for ministry that was so cruelly discarded by the people of North Iowa was later massively received and celebrated in the rest of America. Kathryn would eventually utilize radio, television, and books to inspire multitudes of Christians worldwide to deepen their consecration to Jesus Christ. According to the Kathryn Kuhlman Foundation, which was established in 1954, fifty radio stations eventually carried her thirty-minute broadcasts five days a week, covering most of the United States. These programs were also broadcast into Canada and overseas, reaching much of Europe. Kathryn's weekly half-hour television program, *I Believe in Miracles*, was shown throughout the United States and Canada for a number of years. Many of her television programs and radio sermons can still be seen and heard by way of television and the Internet and many accounts of healings and miracles as a result of her ministry were published in her books and shared on her programs to be remembered for generations to come.

Due to her courage and perseverance, the favor and success that Kathryn experienced in her latter years of ministry would easily eclipse the struggles of her earlier years. These words of Kathryn have been preserved by her foundation as an inspiration to us all: "Living with faith and courage is something that life requires of each of us. Absolutely never give up! Never give in, no matter what! Fight it through! And I promise you something with all of my heart — God will help you."

Even to this day, Kathryn Kuhlman continues to be loved and esteemed by untold numbers of people whose lives and families were touched by her anointing during her lifetime. Her enduring legacy declares all the louder, *"I can do all things through Christ which strengtheneth me"* (Philippians 4:13, KJV). Kathryn's years at Radio Chapel are dynamic proof that, as the Heavens are higher than the earth, the Lord's thoughts and ways are higher than man's. Furthermore, God will always put His might behind the hearts of those who trust Him, and He will empower them with both the strength and ability required to overcome.

"The Heavenly Father does not ask for golden vessels," Kathryn once said. "He does not ask for silver vessels. God asks for yielded vessels — those who will submit their will to the will of the Father. And the greatest human attainment in all the world is for a life to be so surrendered to Him that the Name of God Almighty will be glorified through that life."

About the Author

Shane Philpott is a pastor, speaker, and author who pioneered Christian Fellowship Church in Mason City, Iowa in 1993. He also travels as an itinerate preacher, bringing encouragement to churches and conferences throughout the nation with the purpose of strengthening both leaders and believers. Shane considers it an honor to be the friend of pastors and ministers throughout America, and his highest priority is the edification of Christians.

He is a passionate communicator whose energy, enthusiasm, and humor demonstrate a unique and original approach to ministry. Shane has dedicated his life to helping people put into action the tools, strategies, and attitudes required to produce results in their lives and ministries. He believes in the power of extraordinary vision and the rewards of great faith — a contagious theme that permeates his ministry.

Shane has produced several television programs including *Faith In Action* for CBS as well as *The Dreamer Cometh* for the TCT Network and has additionally appeared as a guest on numerous Christian networks. He is the president of Shane Philpott Ministries and the founder of *preacher2preacher*, an international outreach to those in the five-fold ministry. Shane has authored numerous articles for publication and conducts national webcasts for Christians.

Shane and his wife, Lisa, reside in Mason City, Iowa and are the parents of six children, four of whom were adopted from China.

Contact Information

Website: www.shanephilpott.org

Facebook: www.facebook.com/shanephilpottspm

Email: sphilpott@cf-church.org

PRAYER OF SALVATION

God loves you—no matter who you are, no matter what your past. God loves you so much that He gave His one and only begotten Son for you. The Bible tells us that "...whoever believes in Him shall not perish but have eternal life" (John 3:16 NIV). Jesus laid down His life and rose again so that we could spend eternity with Him in heaven and experience His absolute best on earth. If you would like to receive Jesus into your life, say the following prayer out loud and mean it from your heart.

Heavenly Father, I come to You admitting that I am a sinner. Right now, I choose to turn away from sin, and I ask You to cleanse me of all unrighteousness. I believe that Your Son, Jesus, died on the cross to take away my sins. I also believe that He rose again from the dead so that I might be forgiven of my sins and made righteous through faith in Him. I call upon the name of Jesus Christ to be the Savior and Lord of my life. Jesus, I choose to follow You and ask that You fill me with the power of the Holy Spirit. I declare that right now I am a child of God. I am free from sin and full of the right-eousness of God. I am saved in Jesus' name. Amen.

If you prayed this prayer to receive Jesus Christ as your Savior for the first time, please contact us on the Web at **www.harrisonhouse.com** to receive a free book.

Or you may write to us at
Harrison House • P.O. Box 35035 • Tulsa, Oklahoma 74153

The Harrison House Vision

Proclaiming the truth and the power

Of the Gospel of Jesus Christ

With excellence;

Challenging Christians to

Live victoriously,

Grow spiritually,

Know God intimately.

Kathryn Kuhlman Limited Edition Commemorative Print

Kathryn Kuhlman

This limited edition commemorative print was commissioned to celebrate the enduring legacy of Kathryn Kuhlman and her Radio Chapel years. Each 12" x 15" collectable print comes numbered with a Certificate of Authenticity and is shipped ready for framing.

Visit **www.shanephilpott.org** for more information.

The Story Behind the Story of
Kathryn Kuhlman: The Radio Chapel Years

This DVD is a video narrated and produced by Pastor Shane Philpott, author of *Kathryn Kuhlman: The Radio Chapel Years*, which tells the incredible behind the scenes story of the present-day natural and supernatural events that took place which led to the inspiration for the writing of this book.

Visit **www.shanephilpott.org** for more information.